The Romantic Herb Garden

The Romantic Herb Garden

Caroline Holmes

UNIVERSE

The Romantic Herb Garden
Caroline Holmes

First published in the United States of America in 2004 by
UNIVERSE PUBLISHING
A Division of Rizzoli International Publications, Inc.
300 Park Avenue South
New York, NY 10010
www.rizzoliusa.com

First published as *A Zest for Herbs* in 2004 by
Mitchell Beazley, an imprint of Octopus Publishing Group Ltd,
2–4 Heron Quays, London E14 4JP

Library of Congress Catalog Control Number: 2003114766
ISBN: 0-7893-1047-3

Executive Art Editor Sarah Rock
Commisioning Editor Michèle Byam
Editor Jane Chapman
Design CHK Design
Illustrated Plans Russell Bell
Picture Researcher Emma O'Neill
Production Controller Sarah Rogers
Indexer Sue Farr

Printed and bound in China by
Toppan Printing Company Limited

half-title page: Marigold in midsummer.
title page: Aquilegias, *Rosa* 'Penelope', *Rosa* 'Zéphirine Drouhin',
sweet cicely, *Alchemilla mollis*, Thymus ' 'Fragrantissimus';
design Caroline Holmes
contents page: Mixed planting at Sooke Harbour House,
Vancouver Island, Canada.

Contents

Using Herbs

Good sense tells you there is more to herbs than green leaves. Herbs bring drama and bite to gardens large or small, imparting fragrance and calm, as well as zest to beds and borders. Herbs offer instant effect, providing colour and texture, while other planting schemes mature. They transform small yards, paving, walls, and roof gardens, in full sun or shade.

All native plants are effectively herbs with a kaleidoscopic range of uses, some still relevant today, others splendidly arcane. Add to this palette introduced plants that have naturalized. How do you ascertain such well-adapted plants? Just take a walk on the wild side: head for the countryside or seaside, and investigate local gardens or parks to see what's growing there. Note which plants you like and which ones thrive, then delve into their finer characteristics and ornamental relations. Wormwood evokes bitter medicine, while its latin name, *Artemisia*, represents classical elegance.

What is a herb? The 17th-century apothecary John Parkinson had the perfect definition: "any plant fit for use or delight". I also like the 9th-century description: "praise of cooks and friend of the physician". These useful and delightful herbs have leaves in many shades and variegations that can improve your food and your health. "Herb" describes an extraordinary range of plants from small-leafed creeping mints to evergreen trees.

A common misconception is that all herbs are sun-loving plants. While Mediterranean dwellers including bay, hyssop, lavender, rosemary, and thyme do indeed thrive on dry, sunny terraces, and rosemary and sage will flourish together in a terracotta pot, others perform better in a shaded spot. Mints love damp and some shade, while sweet violets and ivies will colonize dry, shady sites. These moisture- and shade-loving varieties can soon become invasive, however, so plant them where they won't smother other plants.

Herbs offer the gardener a myriad of options. Introduce them as a colour foil, a cushion edging, or a clipped hedge, or use them to deter predators or eradicate weeds. Evergreen herbs such as bay, myrtle, and rosemary offer year-round interest and can be trained or clipped. Summer is peak season but spring herbs will nestle attractively with bulbs, and autumn can be transformed into an Indian summer with a second flush from summer-pruned santolinas and lavenders.

The chessboard with its regular squares remains the ideal layout for a utilitarian plot – for the cook, the craftsmen, the perfumer, or the herbalist. A knot of herbs is an eye-catching and aromatic alternative to box edging. A chamomile seat exuding its fresh apple scent along a wall top or in an arbour is far more appealing than grass, stone, or wood. Toned colour drifts of plants would be lost without the silver billowing of artemisias, santolinas, or helichrysum. Scented roses and lilies are handsomely offset by the soft, almost luminescent edgings of lavender, catmint, or purple sage. Use herbs to create stepping stones in the garden: chamomile steps or swaying beds of coriander, caraway, and baby carrots designed across a terrace or lawn.

Herbs, of course, are also prized for their culinary and medicinal uses. And remember, harvesting your herbs cuts down on maintenance time. Basil and tomatoes thrive together in the ground and enhance each other's appearance on the plate: green with red, purple with yellow – a much-used salad combination that has lost none of its zest. Mint sauce is a traditional accompaniment to lamb, and developed because sheep on Romney Marsh in Kent grazed on wild mint, which flavoured their flesh. Sage has long been served with pork, goose, or cheese because it aids digestion and prevents wind.

Herbs offer an array of different tastes, gently imparting their flavours in the bay leaf-based bouquet garni or in a mixture such as

Previous pages
Golden marjoram flowers and crinkly leaves combine with dandelion and chives to create a wild-meadow planting in just a crack in the paving. It might be too dry for chives, so try a *Festuca* grass instead.

Opposite top
The "Diversity in the Landscape" scheme at Ryton Organic Gardens near Coventry, Warwickshire, shows how mixing herbs such as yarrow, red valerian (*Centranthus*), santolina, and bistort with broom, *Perovskia*, and *Buddleja* is visually pleasing, as well as being ecologically valuable.

Opposite below
Ivy and herbs have long been partners, and here the sculptural topiary, a recent award winner at the Philadelphia Flower Show, looks like it is dancing to the music of thyme. Balanced feeding is essential to ensure even growth throughout the cavorting figure.

herbes provençales — bay leaves, thyme, marjoram, and parsley with basil, chervil, French tarragon, hyssop, lavender, and savory. If time is short, a month or two from late spring onwards is enough to harvest catch crops of chervil, rocket, coriander, and dill.

Such fresh green leaves mixed with salad vegetables give a "bite", along with Chinese and fine chives, lovage, or buckler-leafed sorrel, decorated with edible flowers, including chive florets, nutty rocket flowers, honey borage stars, clear aniseed-tasting fennel umbels, and golden marigold petals. Herbs with aromatic seeds such as cilantro, dill, aniseed, caraway, and fennel can be harvested or left to self-set.

Not only can you graze through your plot but running your hands through the shrubby herbs releases wonderful scents that awaken your senses. Herbs are best planted young and small. Many are raised from seed or cuttings and will give a good display in their first year of planting. They grow rapidly, dressing the garden while slower-growing species are settling in.

Use annual culinary and scented herbs when creating a new bed or renovating an old one because this gives you more chance to clear and feed the soil while enjoying a crop. One of the best to sow in late spring is fiddleneck (*Phacelia tanacetifolia*), whose lavender-blue, nectar-rich flowers attract bees into the garden. Within 16 weeks of sowing you can use the crop as an excellent green manure. Just as the flowers are finishing, cut it back to the ground and leave it to wilt for a couple of days, then dig the whole plant into the ground. An alternative is to sow white sweet clover on a one-year cycle as a green manure — not only does it improve the soil but it also deters mice!

Cultivating the taste for herbs is paramount, so plant or pot a selection such as bay, chives, marjoram, parsley, rosemary, sage, savory, French tarragon, and thyme near an outside door. Enjoy watching them grow and then take pleasure in using them.

Feasting Your Eyes

Creating a visually pleasing scheme, whatever size your garden, is essentially a matter of personal taste. It is about choosing designs and plants that give you most pleasure and reflect your personality – while at the same time hopefully being open to bright new ideas. Imposing a sense of order fulfils this for many, order implying formalities such as symmetry expressed in geometric layouts, clipped hedging, topiary, and gravel, or paving in small spaces. In larger areas this theme is extended with architectural features and sculpture mirrored by stone-edged pools. For others the informality of asymmetrical planting – hardy trees and shrubs, billowing grasses, and wild flowers, water trickling, falling, and or forming limpid pools, and shady secret corners – counteracts the rigidity and regimentation of everyday life.

Introducing herbs to your schemes will enable you to have nature perfected formally or nature as art informally. Hedging herbs such as lavender and santolina can be clipped to provide a broad ribbon around indulgent, voluptuous plantings of flowers and herbs that are best presented like a bouquet – paeonies, lilies, mints, geraniums. Faced with a large expanse of gravel that invited wheelies from visiting cars, I designed a central oval-shaped bed edged in brick and bergenias, and with massed planting of hardy geraniums, paeonies, and lilies – practical, attractive, and scented.

What are the local hard materials that surround you – grey or pink granite; red or cream bricks; shiny flint; white marble? Do they set the colour theme? Do you want a harmonious or contrasting mixture? Clever use of paint and trelliswork can create illusions of space, add architectural interest, and provide extra light. Herbs can be sculpted in imitation or as light relief, drawing the eye along a straight primary or lateral axis, or from side to side as one mound of herbs crosses and contrasts with other planting.

On a grey day, golden-leaved herbs and shrubs provide essential colour and warmth in the garden, as do yellow and orange flowers. Once established, the French marigold (*Calendula officinalis*) seeds

itself, giving flowers almost year round. The petals also brighten up salads as well as being good for you. At Dumbarton Oaks, Washington D.C., this colourful idea has been expanded by planting an *Acer platanoides* at the base of the double herbaceous borders. In autumn, as the chrysanthemums strike gold and red notes, the yellowing acer acts as a crescendo that gradually falls, with the leaves creating a golden pool finale. This effect could be copied on a smaller scale with one of the Japanese acers, or, in light shade, with the fragrant, golden-leaved *Philadelphus coronarius* 'Aureus'. The scent of philadelphus carries well in damp weather, including heavy rain – perfect for a wet summer. On a sunny site, golden bay, *Laurus nobilis* 'Aurea', provides a noble golden note but no pool of leaves as it is evergreen. The golden bay is hardier than the sweet bay, and its leaves are just as good for cooking.

The golden-leaved origanums and thymes are at their best as the days lengthen and warm, the yellow tones calm to fresh greens. Both establish quickly and are good for ground cover and edging. Golden-leaved feverfew, *Tanacetum parthenium* 'Aureum', like all its varieties, grows abundantly and self-seeds with alacrity, the mass of fern-like golden leaves topped with a profusion of daisy flowers providing instant effect. The seedlings are easy to recognize and weed out. In a small garden where such attentions are feasible just cut back after flowering so that it cannot set seeds. The same treatment applies to the golden-variegated lemon balm, *Melissa officinalis* 'Aurea'; its vivid colouring fades as it starts to flower but it will take regular clipping and maintain a globular shape. Recent research has endorsed the Tudor advice that eating lemon balm helps concentration and staves off melancholy – just chop it into your salads. Annually the golden purslane provides a succulent look (and a crunchy addition to a salad), and the tender lemon basil offers a very light delicate green.

Lawrence Johnston's mid-20th-century "Red Border" at Hidcote Manor in Gloucestershire still looks good, threading deep purple-leaved shrubs and plants with red flowers. Purple leaves and flowers are commonly available in herbs: the purple-leaved form of the British native elderflower (*Sambucus* spp.) produces good crops of muscat-scented flowers and berries rich in vitamin C. Another purple choice is *Corylus maxima* 'Purpurea', which offers textural purple foliage, purple catkins, and excellent cob nuts. In an urban setting light-coloured walls provide a perfect backdrop for purple foliage. Introduce gradations of colour with the lighter purple-leaved sage, deep-purple basil and perilla, and frothy purple-flowered hyssop weaving around a dwarf *Berberis thunbergii* 'Atropurpurea Nana'.

The pretty route would be to introduce pink flowers – roses, dianthus, and cosmos; herbs such as the coneflower (*Echinacea*); and pink-flowering varieties of lavender, nepeta, and hyssop. The dramatic alternative would be contrast, using the lime greens of *Euphorbia* such as *E. palustris* and *E. characias* ssp. *wulfenii* (said to deter moles) and *Nicotiana*, especially *N.* x *sanderae* 'Lime Green'. On a smaller scale, try two ancient medicinal herbs: the brilliant golden-leaved *Valeriana phu* and the blue-flowering lungworts such as *Pulmonaria* 'Barfield Regalia', *P.* 'Beth's Blue', and *P.* 'Blue Ensign', which make a late-spring and early-summer show.

There are several herbs that can stand up with other fiery red flowers: many tender salvias such as *S. rutilans* with a pineapple scent and *S. elegans* with a blackcurrant scent; the tropaeolums that include the edible nasturtium – with *T. majus* 'Empress of India' bearing especially deep-red flowers – and the scrambling perennial Scottish flame flower (*T. speciosum*), which will bejewel a dark yew hedge. Also known as bee balm, *Monarda* 'Cambridge Scarlet' is frequently featured in large borders, its shaggy red flowers forming whorls around the square stems. Nor should we forget the lovers' red, clove-scented carnations and red pinks, or the near-black sweet Williams

(*Dianthus barbatus* Nigrescens Group). In winter the valiant *Daphne mezereum* provides scent and colour.

Reds and oranges visually "warm up" a scheme and advance towards the eye. If you are lucky enough to have a westerly aspect, make the most of the setting sun, both in the sky and on your patch, by using reds, oranges, and golds; the effects will be most dramatic in late summer. Blues and whites appear to recede from the eye and have a cooling, calming effect on the viewer. For this reason, blues are valuable in smaller spaces where they give an impression of perspective and depth to a flower border, either in a toned display or when contrasted with yellows. Blues are perceived best at midday, so think about when you look at your garden the most. With its bristly foliage topped by honey-scented blue stars, borage is a must for the summer garden.

Silvers and whites are the most relaxing colours for the eye and lighten up the garden. The bush and compact form, *Helichrysum angustifolium* syn. *H. italicum*, have elegant silvery-white leaves. They must be pruned back to their basal buds every year to prevent them from becoming a floppy mess. The artemisias have produced three gorgeous leafy varieties: *A. absinthium* 'Lambrook Silver' and '*A. a.* 'Powys Castle' are both very hardy with feathery silver foliage, while *A. ludoviciana* bears silver-grey, lance-shaped leaves. They make wonderful foils for red poppies and red-flowering runner beans, and fillers for pink and light-blue schemes. Pink roses underplanted with the silvery haze of pink-flowering lavender or the silver-grey, lemon-scented (*Thymus* x *citriodorus* 'Fragrantissimus') creates a party-frock look.

On moonlit evenings your eyes can tour the garden following the luminous mounds and spikes provided by silver, grey, and purple-leaved herbs. A white garden at night is often scented, as the white flowers exude their fragrance to attract pollinators. How appropriate that the most famous White Garden is at Sissinghurst, in Kent, where the family walked through the garden each evening to gather for supper.

Encouraging visitors such as bees and butterflies will add another layer to the tapestry of your garden. Birds will arrive to feast on elder and cosmos, and you could add to their menu by planting sunflowers. *Buddleja davidii* is a magnet for butterflies, and comes in many shades from white through to deep purple; the yellow-flowering *B. globosa* attracts bees. To add the butterfly dimension in blue and silver schemes, include *Caryopteris* x *clandonensis*, *Heliotropium* cultivars, *Hyssopus officinalis*, lavenders, and *Thymus vulgaris* 'Silver Posie'. Happily, in purple and pink designs, the pinks in herbs tend not to be strident; use soapwort (which provides a welcome mass of ragged pink flowers from late summer), hyssop, lavenders, and *Sedum spectabile*, and then create height with a canopy of honeysuckle.

Two famous 20th-century gardeners, Gertrude Jekyll in England and the painter Claude Monet in France, independently created their hallmark styles of impressionistic drifts of plants. Both were consummate plantspeople who despite poor eyesight would instantly spot a dead flowerhead breaking the colour rhythm of their drifts. Through Jekyll's books and Monet's paintings we can still enjoy the results of their work. Both used herbs extensively throughout their gardens and on their tables – living well into their eighties. Today, with limited space, we can capture their zest and experimental enthusiasm to hone our own skills for new and innovative plantings with herbs.

Total Fragrance

When it comes to aromatic herbs, you are spoilt for choice, and their presence gently pervades the atmosphere. They are the original air fresheners, offering total fragrance not some synthetic replica. In summer, their warm scent is an integral part of balmy memories; after autumnal and winter rains herbaceous herbs, such as the origanums, exude an aroma that is traditionally associated with happiness.

There is an abundance of scents on offer: clear, clean lemon, mint, eucalyptus, and aniseed; fruity apple, pineapple, or strawberry; heady jasmine, orange, rose, or clove – wine- and tea-tasting are nothing in comparison to developing a perfumer's nose. Research carried out by the Oxford Botanical Garden into fragrance has found that we may have three primary colours but there are over a thousand "primary scents". The average human nose has a thousand different types of scent-receptor cells and ten-million receptors in total – figures that fill you with wonder at your own anatomy. Plants, especially through their flowers – and to a lesser extent their leaves, bark, and roots – are perfumed to attract pollinators and to draw or deter predators. Lavenders, sages, and thymes attract honey bees, which we need to pollinate our fruit trees. The eucalpytol scent in eucalyptus deters mosquitoes and, in santolina, clothes moths. The menthol in pennyroyal discourages ants and flies – let it run along shady cracks and crevices, and then pick it when you want to eat outside in a flyless zone. You might also investigate two camphor-scented herbs: balm of Gilead (*Cedronella canariensis*), and camphor alecost (*Tanacetum balsamita*). The former is half-hardy, the latter can be invasive, so choose which one is right for your requirements.

How do you want to savour such delights? In a still, sheltered place, plant scented and aromatic shrubs and herbs under a window or in a window box. Try to have at least one herb such as rosemary or lavender by an entrance so that you can squeeze the leaves as you pass. Prune lavenders to a bud, once they have established. Some varieties will not reshoot from old wood, so if a branch gets broken or you

want to do some heavy pruning you could end up with a collection of dead twigs. Choose a corner of the garden that is upwind, or should I say "upzephyr", so that the heady air comes to you. We have a fragrant wild honeysuckle in our hedge, and its scent wafts across the lane much to our chagrin but to the delight of passing walkers.

With its billowing roses, lilies, sweet peas, and herbs, the old-fashioned cottage garden is a perennial favourite. This informal style of garden is a feast for the senses and begs for an arbour and seat or, at least, a trellis laden with entwined honeysuckle and roses, both of which have medicinal and edible uses. Allow tall lavenders such as *Lavandula* x *allardii* or *L. angustifolia* to tumble over a path backed by the oldest of lilies, *Lilium candidum*.

The cottage garden is my kind of private space, its gentle exuberance embraces you and allows you to stay unseen. It is the ideal style for the gardener who likes to potter for an hour or two, hand weeding and hard pruning as and when is necessary. Hand weeding means getting among your shrubs, flowers, and herbs, and releasing their scents while discovering serendipitous seedlings and ruthlessly eliminating plants in the wrong place. The good news when weeding herbs is, if in doubt about whether a seedling is desirable or not, the resultant smell from a gentle rub will confirm its status.

However, if you want a clean-cut, focused garden hard landscaped with just the sculptural detail of planting, you need not be bereft of fragrance. The watchwords are wall-trained not rambling, ordered not rampant – such precision lies in the hands of the gardener. Standard roses can be created out of any variety; if you want formality, choose a climbing rose such as the heady Fragrant Cloud ('Tanellis'), and order it in advance so that you can have it budded at 1.8m (6ft) rather than 1m (3ft). The fashion for smaller standard roses has been fuelled by our desire to be able to drive away with our garden-centre purchases.

Often beautifully scented, wisterias and honeysuckles can also be grown as standards, the former making a small tree that you can sit under. Wisterias are happy in formal or informal settings – the final look lies in the hand of the pruner. For a wonderful lemony aroma, choose the lemon-scented verbena (*Aloysia triphylla*). It requires a sheltered spot but grows beautifully trained as a "lollipop" in a pot. You will have nothing to look at in winter but as the days lengthen and grow warm, the twigs sprout new shoots with elegant lance-shaped leaves.

For garden ponds and pools, water lilies offer an array of forms and colours, and, in the case of *Nymphaea odorata*, the star-like flowers are also scented. The water hawthorn (*Aponogeton distachyos*) has vanilla-scented flowers that look like a cross between a hawthorn and a hyacinth. It deserves to be grown more widely and is delicious in salads, offering the texture of crisp lettuce stalks and the fragrant flavour of white violets. I first sampled water hawthorn at the birthplace of hybridized water lilies – the Latour Marliac nurseries in Temple-sur-Lot, France – where it happily colonizes some of their pools. I have seen it in the Otter Pond at Audley End in Essex and in other water features from the size of a tub to a small lake. If you want it to thrive and be edible ensure the water is kept clean.

With a little planning you can enjoy fragrance all year round. You can retain the summer in a heated conservatory or well-lit house with scented geraniums. Like so many pot plants, they benefit greatly from being put out after the last frosts – not necessarily planted – and sunk into the ground where they can flourish in the natural light and gather minerals from the rains. Scented geraniums are packed with wonderful fragrance, such as the nutmeg-scented *Pelargonium* 'Fragrans', which you can rub on aching feet, and the rose-scented *Pelargonium* 'Graveolens', which can be infused in tea to lift your spirits and improve your circulation. Other scents include lemon, mint, cedar-rose, peach, apple, balsam, and camphor. Search out *P. quercifolium*,

P. 'Radula', *P. tomentosum*, and cultivars with winning names such as 'Clorinda', 'Mabel Grey', and 'Prince of Orange'.

One of the finest winter scents is that of *Lonicera fragrantissma* and *L.* × *purpusii* 'Winter Beauty'– shrubby honeysuckles whose small creamy white flowers dangle from leafless branches in January, February, and March. The orange-flower scent hangs in the winter air; just one or two sprigs, if picked, can fill a room with scent. After flowering both honeysuckles become large green shrubs without the architectural qualities of myrtle, bay, or rosemary, so always combine them with other plantings to maintain year-round interest.

The witch hazel (*Hamamelis mollis*) basks in a sunny site. A dark backdrop of bay or yew allows you to appreciate fully its bare branches punctuated with pretty clusters of deep-yellow, shaggy flowers – at their biggest and best on the cultivar 'Pallida'. On a warm winter day the scent carries quite a distance, and the autumnal leaves curl into attractive shades of yellow. The rampant *Petasites fragrans* is worth consideration if you have a moist area of wild woodland, as its late-winter flowers have an overpowering scent of vanilla. In Japan the plant's deep and extensive root system is widely harvested and eaten.

By combining carefully selected scented bulbs such as snowdrops and crocuses with *Iris histroides*, *I. reticulata*, or *I. unguicularis* you can have scent and colour from late autumn till spring. A bed devoted to these bulbs (excluding *I. unguicularis*) will be free to grow annual herbs, including basil, chervil, and rocket through late spring and summer. An approximate routine should be: mulch in November; start sowing herb seeds in April, and basil in late May; and weed when necessary.

As the green blade rises, herbs join the chorus of fresh new shoots to smell and sample. The sweet violet (*Viola odorata*) will spread into any shady corner and flower abundantly from mid spring; the white-flowering selection is particularly fragrant and delicious in salads. The golden-leaved herbs are especially attractive, providing a background of spring freshness, as the days lengthen. Resist the temptation to plant shrubby herbs until mid spring – drying winds are preferable to late frost or cold damp. The elegant *Iris germanica* var. *florentina* has white flowers with a bluish flush. Its scented rhizomes are the source of orris root powder, which is used in perfumes and cosmetics. The fragrant, single-flowering *Paeonia officinalis* has a long medicinal history as well as being ornamental long after its crimson flowers have died. It is often erroneously written that cats like only *Nepeta cataria* – our cat rolls feverishly in *N. racemosa*, whose scent sends her into ecstasy.

Early summer is total fragrance month for herbs; the days are long, and the inclination to seek out and savour is strong. Old-fashioned pinks (*Dianthus*) include some varieties that are centuries old. The evocatively named 'Sops-in-Wine' has white flowers, zoned deep crimson-purple (try floating it in cold drinks), and 'Mrs Sinkins' has double white flowers. Catherine Sinkins raised this floriferous, fragrant beauty with her husband John Thomas Sinkins, Master of Slough Workhouse in the late 19th century. The ranks of summer perennials are joined by scented biennials such as the evening primrose, (*Oenothera biennis*), and sweet rocket (*Hesperis matronalis*). Tender perennials, including scented geraniums and salvias give fragrant foliage interest and delicate flowers. They will continue throughout the summer into autumn, as the flowering shrubs, roses, and lilies complete their efforts.

As the onset of frost approaches, bringing its own scents, you have to decide where to clear ground for self-sowing and what to lift until the following spring. Breathe in the smell of the damp autumn soil – it has a fragrance all of its own.

Right
Scents in the late-winter garden are to be prized, and among the few herbs that fulfil this promise is *Daphne mezereum*. Formerly an important although deadly extract, mezereon was used medicinally.

Opposite page
The white on the deep pink of the old Gallica rose *Rosa mundi* looks like shot silk, and the medieval setting of feverfew and golden marjoram creates a compatible and pleasurable image.

Do Me a Flavour

Herbs have played an essential role in cookery down the ages, imparting flavour, fragrance, zest, and colour to cooked and raw dishes, as well as being an important food preservative. On warm summer days, gently grazing herbs from all over the garden is a wonderful prelude to food preparation; for colder days, make sure you have a good selection ready harvested. I like to keep a jam jar full of freshly picked herbs such as bay, rosemary, and savory in the kitchen, rather than hanging them up to dry where they can rapidly become dusty and stale.

Good taste
Match your mood and taste buds to the many different flavours on offer. The leaves of fresh mouth-tinglers such as sorrel, mint, and fennel have an appetising effect. The sweet fragrance of marjorams, oregano, and thymes work harmoniously with fresh tomatoes or cooked squashes, chicken, and pasta. Transform bland ingredients into *haute-cuisine* with French tarragon, chervil, parsley, and chives. Enliven bread and fish dishes with the distinctive tastes of dill and fennel seed; the latter imparts an entirely different flavour to that of their zesty leaves. Infuse desserts and other sweet dishes with flavours such as lemon balm, bergamot, sweet cicely, and rosemary.

If you have tried and disliked more unusual herbs, for example, angelica, lovage, salad burnet, or orache, revisit them early in the season, when their leaves are fresh and aromatic, rather than elderly and pungent. Like vegetables, herbs have their peak seasons; unlike them, many are perennial. Many plants are listed as edible but you need to ascertain their window of gourmet possibility, so take regular nibbles throughout the seasons. Lovage can be cut back in midsummer to provide fresh leaves and shoots until knocked back by the cold weather. Golden or purple orache become increasingly unpalatable as they gain height and are beyond use or delight once they become seed-festooned spikes.

Previous pages
Bronze fennel stands guard against the backdrop of Sooke Harbour on Vancouver Island. Warming, aniseed-flavoured fennel is the perfect cooking companion for freshly caught fish. Every plant on view is edible.

Right
Nurserywoman and writer Carol Klein has woven bluebells, columbines, and sweet woodruff under dappled shade. The white, star-like, aromatic woodruff flowers are just ripe for picking.

Below
Mammoth is the largest and most dramatic seed-bearing variety of dill. Here, the seedheads intermingle with the brightly ornamental flowers of the tagetes.

Chives

The grass-like leaves of this member of the alliums are used to flavour a wide range of dishes. As long as your garden enjoys regular rain through the summer, you can cut chive clumps to the ground after flowering – two or even three times in one season. This will ensure a regular supply of fine spikes. Harvest the flowers when they are newly opened; with a deft twist at the base of the flower head, the florets will separate, and can be scattered over food. Do not make the mistake of eating the whole head, as the resultant wave of onion is overpowering.

The shyer flowering garlic or Chinese chives should not be cut right back after flowering, so just harvest the broad, flat spikes when you need them. In late summer you will be rewarded with delightful white flowers, the florets of which are deliciously garlicky. And true garlic is easy to grow: simply choose the biggest cloves to plant on the shortest day of the year – with good sunshine and soil they will be ready for harvest on the longest day.

Parsley

There are essentially three varieties of parsley: the moss-curled and plain-leaved parsleys, and the root-forming Hamburg parsley. The strongest flavour lies in the stems, so when stewing or making sauces add finely chopped stems, reserving the leaves until the last minute or to use as a garnish. Despite its Latin name, *Petroselenium* – meaning "rock celery"– parsley fares best on good alkaline soil but will seed itself onto poor soil or into cracks and crevices. If you want lots of parsley you will have to approach its culture attentively but if you are happy with the occasional picking buy a plant and leave it to self-seed.

There is a wealth of folklore surrounding the sowing and raising of parsley, so just sow at fortnightly intervals from early spring onwards until you succeed. Traditional advice was never to transplant parsley, which is a problem if you plan to buy plants. Simply buy as young a plant as possible for planting out, or sink the pot into prepared ground, then use it as much as possible until flowering and leave it to self-seed. Most pot-grown supermarket parsleys will not thrive if planted out.

Chewing vitamin A- and C-rich parsley leaves cleanses and refreshes the mouth, especially after eating garlic. The moss-curled variety contains a flavonoid, apigenin, which reduces allergic responses, and acts as an anti-oxidant.

Savory

There are two savories: the perennial winter and annual summer varieties. The aromatic leaves have a peppery flavour. Winter savory thrives in a dry, sunny position and is almost indestructible, its hardiness and spiky green leaves making it a valuable filler in borders and beds. It has delicate pink flowers, which appear in late summer. At the Museum of Garden History in London, the bushes have been trained into delightful globes – the more you clip or use savory the better it will be. The soft-stemmed, tender summer savory is delicious chopped on steamed green beans or in bean salads. Sow at the same time as spring broad beans and late-spring/early-summer French, haricot, and runner beans. As the summer advances, the leaves darken, providing a delicate foil for the tiny pink flowers. Once it is established you can ruthlessly eat the stems and flowers right up to the first frosts.

Aromatics

Aroma is usually a good guide to flavour, one exception being the curry-scented helichrysums — you will not be poisoned by using the leaves but the resultant dish is hardly worth the effort. Curry spices should be mixed according to which foods you are preparing; the aromatic seed-bearing herbs such as fennel, coriander, and aniseed are useful, and the fresh leaves of the cilantro coriander are hardy growers. There is also an enormous range of spicy and hot capsicum varieties available to the home gardener. Late-summer Harvest Shows throughout the United States include amazing displays of capsicums, tomatoes, and aubergines (eggplant).

The clean lemony flavour of sorrel is recognizable in a salad but when added to a béchamel sauce it is more akin to the taste of spinach. Two weeds that cook up well early in the year are the slightly fishy-flavoured nettle and the ground elder, which makes a useful spinach substitute in lasagnes and fish pies.

Basil, garlic, and pinenuts processed in olive oil are a well-established combination. If you like your garlic with a punch, try rosemary, garlic, and walnuts in sunflower oil, forked through rice. I know a Greek cook in Pennsylvania who transforms calabrese by dropping it into hot olive oil with finely chopped rosemary and slivers of garlic for a few minutes — it is delicious served with fresh pasta.

Smoky herbs

Whether your heart sinks at the waft of a barbecue or not, twiggy herbs such as rosemary, lavender, thyme, and mature lemon balm can

Below
Variegated applemint and golden marjoram have colonized an enclosed corner of my garden. Bright from spring onwards, their young leaves are excellent in salads and later in the year for cooking.

Opposite page
In late spring sweet cicely flowers fill the gaps of later-flowering shrubs and plants at Greathan Mill in Hampshire. The aniseed-flavoured ferny leaves and white umbels jostle with columbines. Cicely leaves are natural sweeteners for rhubarb.

be put over the burning charcoal to produce the aroma of hot, dry summers. Mature rosemary twigs make attractive skewers for barbecued kebabs, imparting their flavour to the meat, fish, or vegetables. Any ingredients awaiting the barbecue will be improved by an overnight marinade in a herb-enriched oil.

The dill weed is widely used to flavour fish dishes, including the Scandinavian home-cured salmon known as "gravadlax". Dill seeds, meanwhile, are great in pickles. Dill fares best early or later in the season, preferring long nights and cool temperatures. It can be sown from early spring until the end of summer – the final sowing will produce a stunted crop but one that will give you fresh pickings until the frosts start. Dill weed complements salad potatoes, either as a garnish or in an oil drizzle or homemade mayonnaise. In fact I could eat newspaper with dill mayonnaise, it is my undoubted favourite!

Flowers

Herbs are good sources of edible flowers that are both decorative and full of health-enhancing minerals and vitamins. Flowers, including chive florets, fennel umbels, salad rocket, French marigolds, and nasturtiums enliven a salad. Adding elderflower umbels to dishes such as sorbets will impart a muscat flavour. Sweet woodruff adds an essence of cucumber to white wines in late spring and early summer. Some years ago I was a speaker at an iris festival at the Prieuré St. Michel in Normandy. It had been a cool spring, and regrettably there was not a single iris in flower. The culinary day was saved by copious use of flowering woodruff in cold soups, drinks, and sauces.

A Touch of Genius

Hands-on gardeners know just how a good soil should feel – the texture as you hold it in your palm or run it through your fingers, a soil that you can work with or one that needs improving. Once your herbs are growing, you can indulge in their tactile pleasures: running your hands along hedges; rubbing and touching shrubs; and pinching aromatic leaves and petals. Remember, though, that "touch" is the watchword. You should never crush the life out of a leaf or twig in a bid to savour its scent. A gentle press releases the essential oils that in turn leave a scent on your hand. Weeding with a hoe will send up earthy scents and clear the soil, but there are greater advantages still to getting down on your knees. Anyone gardening with herbs should enjoy the gift of free seedlings; as your hand is about to inadvertently weed up a herb favourite, you will quickly smell the error of your ways.

Clipped accents

For me, beautiful herbs leave indelible memories. The solidity of the clipped rosemary hedge that graces the Queen's Garden at the Royal Botanic Gardens, Kew. Or up the hill at Leith Hall in Aberdeenshire, where the visual excitement of clever planting is enhanced by brushing through the cascade of nepetas that line the herbaceous borders. Or the santolinas that curvaceously enclose the flowerbeds on the roof of château d'Angers in the Loire Valley. At the Governor's Palace in Williamsburg, Virginia, the emetic holly, *Ilex vomitaria*, is much used to frame the "ballroom" garden that leads to the wisteria-covered arbour.

As manual dexterity improves, there is the advanced skill of gently weaving wayward honeysuckles and clematis, and training roses and sweet peas. The more you pick sweet peas, the more they will flower and for longer. You can eat the flowers but never the seeds.

Clipped box hedges have been the stalwart of many design fashions: elaborate Italianate and French styles made way for the clean outlines of Modernism, which in turn is being replaced by amorphous shapings such as cloud formations or placing sculptures in a sea of lavender.

Moorish gardens have the simplest of layouts, their intricacies confined to scrolled words and patterns in the surrounding stone or plaster work – poems that invite your fingers to trace out the script. The rectangular pool in the Court of the Myrtles at the Alhambra Palace, in southern Spain, mirrors the sky, the swooping birds, and surrounding architectural details. The pool is edged with clipped hedges of green myrtle, which, as the day warms up, waft a gentle, spicy scent. It is worth noting that Moorish gardens were mostly viewed from sitting positions on cool marble and silks, so think about what you will see and touch when sitting in your garden.

On well-drained soil and in a sunny position rosemary is another fine choice for a hedge. The aromatic evergreen leaves call out to be rubbed to release their aroma. Rosemary also makes an excellent wall shrub, and, although it is not supposed to exceed 1.8m (6ft), the rosemary growing by a friend's south-facing front door has now passed her bedroom windows.

Passing by

Bay trees (*Laurus nobilis*) look handsome throughout the year. Their deep-green, fragrant leaves, which are infinitely touchable, are widely used in cookery, and can be harvested for wreaths and garlands. If you have an open fire, follow tradition and burn your Christmas wreaths on January 6, the Twelfth Day of Christmas – the flames and scent are wonderful. The golden bay (*L. n.* 'Aurea') has golden-yellow leaves.

In sheltered or maritime areas (or in a conservatory), the lemon verbena draws your hand to enjoy its clear lemon scent. The leaves

are quite rough but well worth harvesting for scenting a room.
A smaller, easier-to-grow alternative would be to choose one of
the many scented pelargoniums.

If you are in London, go to the National Portrait Gallery and look
at G.F. Watts' painting of his young bride, Ellen Terry, cupping a
camellia in her hands. With their long history, large, conspicuous
flowers such as camellias and paeonies make natural companions to
herbs. The very act of holding a flower in your palm or between your
fingers concentrates the senses of touch, sight, and smell, so plant
accessible flowers to encourage a hands-on appreciation.

A place to sit

In the herb garden at Sissinghurst, in Kent, old bricks and masonry
were recycled to create Edward the Confessor's seat, effectively a
stone two-seater chesterfield sofa with a cushion of chamomile. The
chamomile used is 'Treneague', a low-growing, non-flowering variety
with a wonderful apple scent. Another "living seat" at Sissinghurst is
in the White Garden, where a plank surrounded by clipped box forms
an elegant garden bench. In the Paradise Garden at Yalding Organic
Gardens, in Kent, I designed two medieval arbours. These are box
seats filled with soil and enclosed by a trellised arbour. The arbours
are swathed in scented honeysuckles and roses, and underplanted with
bulbs and pinks. The seats are formed from a mixture of single- and
double-flowering chamomile, which are hardier than 'Treneague',
and visitors are encouraged to sit on them. The effect is one of gentle
rollering, and the result is a sweet-smelling springy turf with flowers.

The garden adjoining the Museum of Garden History is a haven for Londoners. The public seats have been enclosed in different ways: there is a wooden seat backed by traditional trellis with clematis and two potted agapanthus; a stone bench flanked by two pillar-box myrtles; and two other stone seats, one backed by clipped rosemary and the other by clipped variegated euonymus.

Soft to the touch

Silver and grey schemes are complemented by many herbs, some of which have a velvety pubescence. One of the finest is mullein (*Verbascum thapsus*), which has white or grey woolly foliage and tall flowering spires that add architectural interest. Although mullein self-seeds freely, the good news is that the seedlings are easily recognizable and can be despatched at an early stage. Mullein has many medicinal uses, and, reputedly, wrapping figs in the leaves stops putrefaction! We always eat mine as they ripen, so I have not put this to the test.

Fig leaves offer a tactile sensation – smooth and green on top and bristly underneath; by the time you pick them, the fruits have the smoothest skin stretched across the soft purple flesh. Here in East Anglia the variety 'Brunswick' does superbly well, annually yielding quantities of large pale-green figs. We grow it against our south-east-facing cottage wall in pits lined with paving stones underplanted with rue, which provides an attractive skirt. In the Southern States of the USA, figs are grown in stools, that is a circle with about 8–12 clear trunks.

Betony, also known as Bishop's wort, presumably because it was said to protect you from witchcraft, is the medicinal *Stachys*, a true herb but the least hirsute. We associate the soft mounds of lamb's ears, tails, or tongue (*Stachys byzantina*) with cottage gardens, and there are many superb choices. 'Cotton Ball' is especially woolly, and there are also variegated forms that will soften path and terrace edges. Four notable American species are the sprawling Californian *S. bullata*; the erect north West Coast *S. ciliata*; the softly hirsute Texan *S. coccinea*; and the East Coast pink-flowering hyssop-leaved stachys.

Two other soft-to-the-touch herbs are white horehound (*Marrubium vulgare*) and *Lavandula lanata*, both of which are primarily decorative and need sunny, well-drained positions. Lastly, there is woolly thyme, which grows like a silky carpet across rocks and gravel, flowering with a mass of mauve flowers beloved by bees.

A shady garden haven

"Luscious and comforting shade enlivened by the touch of the sun." This was how Shakespeare described a honeysuckle-canopied arbour. Honeysuckles, wisteria, and clematis entwine arbours, give off scent, and develop sculptural, fissured barks that invite you to touch. Our arbour has purple and white wisterias for spring, and roses and vines for summer; the red grapes are full of pips but there is romantic pleasure in picking them while reading.

A rose-covered arbour always looks romantic. An exquisite choice is the thornless, fragrant Bourbon rose 'Zéphirine Drouhin', which actually does better trained on an arbour or trellis than against a wall. It bears semi-double cerise-pink flowers and reaches a height of 2.5m (9ft) high with a spread of 1.8m (6ft).

Left
The paving, hedging, and planting all create movement in this courtyard designed by Bunny Guinness. The chequerboard effect in the paving is provided by thymes, whose compact growth contrasts with the voluptuous plantings of dahlias and cannas.

Below
In his design for the 2001 Chelsea Flower Show, Michael Miller reinterpreted the chequerboard design into shallow square steps with accompanying boxes of roses and lavender. The garden offers a pleasing combination of textures, which encourages you to reach out and touch.

Sound Health

Rosemary and parsley traditionally thrived where the woman "wore the trousers" or "ruled" – not her household but her garden. The sound health of both herbs indicates a garden in good heart, sunny and well drained as well as fertile and fecund. Eating both herbs will add zest to your step.

Dancing to the music of thyme

A healthy garden buzzes with sounds – just make time to hear them. While listening to the sound of bees, birds, and dragonflies, look at what lies around you. Does the garden's layout beat out the rhythms of country dances or the tranquil sounds of plain song? Can you translate what moves you musically into a growing, tangible design?

Again and again the chequerboard design of a monastic garden is recreated to revive a peaceful spiritual oasis, where the monk's meditative and gardening work was echoed in the exquisitely simple sound of plainsong. Whenever I stand in a cloister or look over simple beds I can sense the pure sound of those voices. Try listening to modern recordings of the music of medieval mystic nun Hildegarde of Bingen, who gardened and composed music as well as writing on theology, natural history, and the healing power of plants.

Gardens should be colourful and capricious expressions of your idiosyncrasies, not simply painted by numbers. You might wish for more romance in the garden, so how about letting songs of undying, chivalrous love blossom with roses, myrtle, carnations, and, the subtle symbols of erotic love, violets?

The Renaissance transformed the medieval flowery meads, bowers, and turf seats as well as the composition and arrangement of music. As grandees wove their gardens into elaborate conceits, their music evolved into textured complexities using more than 20 instruments; singing and dancing also became highly mannered. One gardening book dating from 1616 advises beating turf by dancing on it. The rhythm of the music guided dancing feet into knot and clover leaf

forms, which can be created in herb knots still heard in Van Morrison and The Chieftain's Celtic remake of *Mairi's Wedding*. The knot itself can be elaborate or purely a simple basket weave of rectangular beds arranged in patterns rather than in a row or square. The long summer evenings in Scotland just ask for reels as "…Over hillways, up and down, myrtle green and bracken brown…", or more modestly among the flower borders.

The garden can double as a theatre in which both the setting and music are equally elaborate; herbs can provide the poetry and movement, while seasonal bowers provide shelter for the guitarist or flautist. In my teens Simon and Garfunkel's revival of *Scarborough Fair* put herbs to music; more recently the group Incubus used a key signature that alternates between three-four and four-four time, a pattern reminiscent of the knot garden.

Dietary aid

Dancing and gardening help maintain sound health and control weight gain. Recent research shows that eating thyme may slow down the ageing process. Whether this is true or not, there is no doubt that thyme is an excellent addition to hot and cold foods and tisanes. None of us wants to end up like the vulture in Hilaire Belloc's poem, whose eye was dim and neck was thin from picking between meals. One solution is to chew fennel seed, which anesthetizes the taste buds and arrests the temptation to snack. Traditionally eaten during times of fast, fennel seed gives the mouth a pleasant aniseed buzz. It is a natural digestive, diuretic, and help for lactating mothers.

There is an old saying "plant fennel by your kennel", which is sound advice not just because fennel's scent deters fleas but also because it crosses easily with other umbellifers such as dill, aniseed, and caraway, so they are best kept apart to avoid having beds full of insipid-tasting hybrids. Fortunately it is only fennel that has this habit, although planting dill with carrots is not advised. However, I recommend sowing anise and coriander together. Sweet fennel and bronze fennel are related to Florentine fennel but will never produce a vegetable-sized root.

A garden's wellbeing

What about the health of your garden? Traditionally, chamomile was said to be the "plant's physician", its presence seemingly improving the wellbeing of all plants in the vicinity. Similarly, the profuse lemon balm attracts bees – control its growth by eating it regularly as an intellectual and emotional tonic. As domestic pest and disease treatments are being increasingly restricted and the organic movement grows, it is worth considering the juxtapositioning of plants to deter predators and perhaps improve the microclimate. Many aromatic herbs are excellent deterrents: grow basil with tomatoes, summer savory with peas or beans. And it is far better to have earwigs and black fly on your nasturtium flowers than on your roses, dahlias, or beans.

Thymes and alliums are both recommended as pest deterrents for roses, thymes faring best with rambling and rugosa roses that grow in poor soils. At Drum Castle in Aberdeenshire they have created a carpet of golden thyme under the Gallica roses. Alliums, including chives, come in a variety of flower colours and will enjoy the rich soil of hybrid tea and standard roses, as will garlic, although the effect with them will be less ornamental. The spurges are known for their milky white sap, which is toxic internally, and a serious skin irritant externally. In flowerbeds and borders, however, the violently purgative caper or mole spurge (*Euphorbia lathyris*) reputedly deters moles.

Other recommended combinations include borage with tomatoes, pumpkins, squashes, and strawberries; borage leaves are added to many cold drinks, including Pimms. Mildew will show on hyssop before it hits your vines, and marigolds, the *Calendula* or *Tagetes* varieties, deter pests from tomatoes, cucumber, and asparagus. Mints will thrive as an underplanting for raspberries, and the pennyroyal repels mosquitoes, ants, and flies. Cats will seek out catnip (*Nepeta*), which is also said to be a deterrent to flea beetle and mice.

Enter your garden with a heart "merrie and joyful" by including a medlar tree underplanted with meadowsweet, a combination that was said to give your garden magic qualities. With your senses awakened, how can the garden be anything but magic?

Opposite page
The gardens at Sooke Harbour House on Vancouver Island provide a seasoned landscape, with every plant on show edible. Herbs and vegetables required in larger quantities are raised in beds edged with blue boards, combining utility with beauty.

Below
The apothecary's rose, *Rosa gallica* var. *officinalis*, whose flowers promote healing, improve your morale and are used to control bacterial infections. The soft petals can be scattered over salads and puddings – so eat up and say goodbye to lethargy!

Infusing Style

Just as tisanes can be infusions of mint, chamomile, or ginger, herbs in the garden can infuse styles and emotions, while remaining firmly rooted in the soil. It is the plants that prove whether the two-dimensional plan that looks so good on paper translates into a three-dimensional form. Herbs can make a garden move and billow, or assail the senses.

Gardeners looking to create a formal style should work within a square grid or a circle. When you come to design your abstract patchwork, inner knot, or parterre, make it simple in small areas and increasingly elaborate in larger areas. Geometric repetition can be as eye-catching as the intricate flourishings and branchings of French formal-style gardens; a chessboard of different thymes underplanted with early winter bulbs gives year-round pleasure. The marriage of Tudor and Art Deco styles at Eltham Palace in south-east London is encapsulated in the triangular area between the 1930s' extension and the moat, where a brick lattice pattern outlines block plantings of sage, thyme, and phormium.

If you have an area of garden near a sliding door, ease the transition from inside to out by mixing paving with flat or cushioned plantings, then use a wall-trained shrub or clipped bay to give height. Just outside Chepstow on the Welsh Borders there is a modern house and garden, where the paving, planting, and grass create a good transitional pattern. Providing height with a difference and casting interesting shadows is a redundant railway signal. When putting in a vertical feature, consider where it will cast its shadow and how the sun will catch it. Alternate the planted areas with a mixture of hard textures – bricks, paving, pebbles, mosaic, and a pool or basin.

Entering the garden down steps from the house begs for different treatment. For a traditional look, use hazy lavender hedging and soft edgings of lamb's ears. Alternatively, you can dramatize the effect with minimalist planting. For this, the stone or brickwork needs to have clean lines styled with simple herb topiary or blocks of silver-leaved thyme.

Previous pages
At Hidcote Manor in Gloucestershire
the stone edge of the pool ensures that the
cotton lavender is rooted in dry soil, while
draping dramatically over the water.

Opposite page
At the Instituto Moraira Salles in Brazil,
Roberto Burle Marx used abstract shapes
to create dynamic curvaceous and angular
planting plans.

Above
Resembling an expanse of water, drifts
of the English lavender (*Lavandula
angustifolia* 'Little Lady') provide sheets
of colour flowing and flowering under
and through the weeping pear at Hampton
Court in Herefordshire.

Following pages
The vivid green of moss-curled parsley
delightfully edges beds of bright yellow
rudbeckias at West Dean Gardens in Sussex.

Drifters

To create a seemingly random drift of herbs to run in and around other plantings, literally throw compost and sand into sweeping arcs, which you can then either sow or plant up. If you have a new garden, a year growing a green manure such as fiddleneck (*Phacelia tanacetifolia*) gives you time to plan, as well as breaking up and clearing the soil. There is also the added bonus of soft, lavender, nectar-rich blooms which attract bees. Thereafter you can play with succession sowings of nasturtiums, cilantro coriander, dill, chervil, or summer savory to fill in any gaps as green foils for night-scented stock or cerinthe.

When you have cleared the ground, ensure it is free of perennial weeds. If you have time, it is worth styling your proposed formal or informal shapes with annual herbs. This gives you a chance to test whether your ideas will work and an extra opportunity to dig the site over. Mint thrives in a moist, shady site, so restrict its growth by planting it in a bucket or with slates around it and re-plant each year to ensure beautifully shaped mints that stay in one place. As well as green-leaved mints, there are also purple, gold, and white-variegated forms with scents ranging from peppermint to eau de cologne.

Slopes

Lesser celandines, also known as pilewort because of their medicinal use for hemorrhoids, provide a spring carpet under deciduous shrubs and herbaceous perennials. They are invasive but easily recognizable and removable when it is interesting to note their adherence to the "Doctrine of Signatures", that is the traditional belief that every plant carries a sign that indicates its use. Beth Chatto has used celandines spectacularly under the trees that lead to her water garden. I let the greater celandine self-seed as its glaucous, grey-green foliage billows under my roses and alongside the hemerocallis; as the season advances I weed them out, leaving just a few to set seed.

Simple but effective is a terracotta pot of rosemary underplanted with sage, which infuses style and your tea.

Instant & Long-term Effect

Successful transplanting of specimen and mature plants requires tender, loving care, if they are to thrive and grow without suffering a check on their growth. Buying containerized plants makes this possible. If you do choose to buy well-established plants ensure that they are not root bound. A cursory glance at the base of the pot will let you know: if there is a tangled weave of roots under the base, you will almost undoubtedly find that the roots within the pot are similarly cramped. Unless you ease the roots apart, and trim to encourage new growth, the plant will continue to push roots into this complex circular system rather than delving for the goodies in the soil. If you have to do radical root pruning you will have to match it on top, thus defeating the advantages of instant effect.

A specimen whose roots are just visible around the holes in the pot base is settled and ready to face the big wide world. It is still worth easing the roots apart, as this encourages them to venture outwards; the younger the root the more hairs it has and the easier it will draw up water and nutrients. Make the planting hole larger than the root ball and fill with fibrous compost to encourage good root development; if space is at a premium, cut the roots back so that they are considerably smaller than the space available.

Small is beautiful

You may not get instant effect but I would always recommend starting with young, smaller plants, as they are more adaptable, and I guarantee that within five years they will be looking just as good as the more mature starters. They adapt better to climatic vagaries, need little or no staking, and are unlikely to suffer from windrock. After planting in autumn, regularly check that the soil remains firm around the plants, as frost will penetrate straight to the root down any gaps and fissures. Autumn is a good time for some economy hedging work: dwarf box

Plan for Immediate Impact

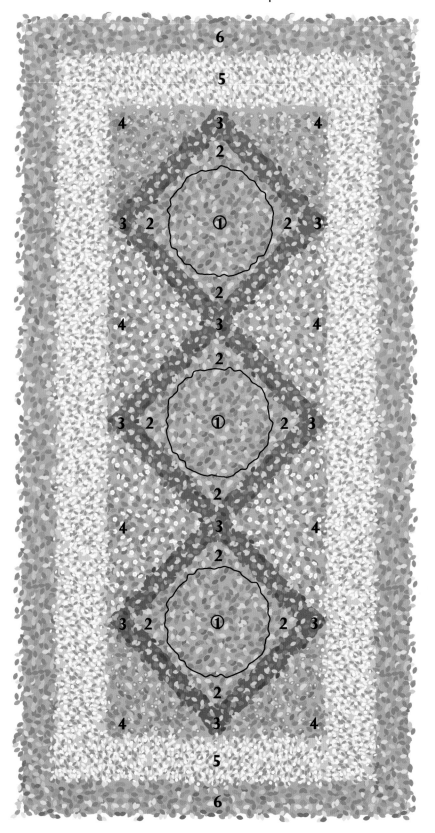

Key

1   Central 3 features
2   Underplanting around 1
3   Diaper hedging
4   Underplanting outside diaper hedging
5   Inner of outer 2 hedges
6   Final outer hedge

Plant list

1   Sweet bay or willow-leaved pear or flowering crab apple, or Japanese cherry

2   Bergenia or double-flowering lawn chamomile or the thymes 'Archer's Gold', 'Silver Posie', and orange scented

3   Annuals – bush basil or stump-rooted carrots or German chamomile

4   Coneflower or blue-flowering hyssop

5   Neapolitan cotton lavender or lavender 'Grosso'

6   Dwarf box

and lavender will root well from cuttings placed in situ. Prepare a planting trench in whatever pattern you want to have your final hedge. It is worth investing in about 10 good pots of box or lavender, and planting them at key points in the design. Take 10cm (4in) heel cuttings and push them into the prepared soil, with added sharp sand for drainage and compost for fibre. By spring, you should have an 80-percent take and the embryo outlines of your herbal boundary.

Having selected your specimen shrubs – which might include large herbs such as bay trees and myrtle – you can surround them with truly instant-effect herbs. Perennials, including thymes, chives, and marjorams, and annuals such as summer savory, chervil, and parsley will cover the bare earth with waves of useful leaves. Thugs, including the jungle herbs angelica, lovage, and sweet cicely, and cushion-formers such as lemon balm, mints, and soapwort colonize speedily but need to be kept in check.

Annuals

Why sow herb seeds rather than bedding flowers? Apart from the harvest, you can stagger your effects, create temporary patterns, and sow into any gaps. Remember that in nature seeds fall onto soft but firm ground, so tread newly-dug ground if you are sowing outside; if sowing inside press the compost into your seed trays. Cover seeds with their own depth of compost – small seeds such as basil need only a sprinkling but large seeds, including nasturtium, require about 1cm (⁄in). On the adjoining plan the diaper planting numbered 3 is for immediate impact using annual herbs. I have suggested bush basil, German chamomile, or stump-rooted carrots, but any small-leaved herb such as the sweet marjoram, which is treated as an annual, would be ideal. In a kitchen garden you could try lettuces, ornamental cabbages, French beans, or summer savory. Seeds sown directly into the ground will "hold" longer before transplanting or thinning; if you have space you might want to sow a small selection in a "holding" bed so that you can have extra herbs to drop in later on. Sweet peas climb through early flowering shrubs and herbaceous perennials to lengthen the season.

Perennials

The fact that many herbs are short-lived makes them perfect for larger schemes. While box hedging is maturing, try lining it with the quicker-growing cotton or ordinary lavenders (*see the plan on the opposite page*). They will look good in the first year, and great in the second and subsequent five to ten years; as the box matures it will provide a clean green edge to the more ragged bases of the lavender. Hyssop is a perennial that seeds itself every year but even with vigorous pruning in spring the parent plant needs replacing every five years.

Sages, lawn chamomile, and cushion and creeping thymes root easily from cuttings. There are two methods of rooting and renewal. Firstly, in autumn, gently sprinkle a fibrous compost over the stems up to the bottom leaves; by spring the old bare stems will be a mass of young rootlets. Lift and cut off the old root system, and replant. Alternatively, you can take tip cuttings in early summer and root them in a propagator, where they should root within six weeks. Harden them off, and either pot them up for spring planting or plant in early autumn.

The coneflowers (*Echinacea* spp.) have attracted growing publicity in recent years due to their medicinal potential. They have wonderful large, daisy-like flowers and take their name from their dark, prickly, teasel-like centres. *Echinos* is the Greek for a hedgehog or sea urchin. They are remarkably tough and will withstand heat with high humidity, drought, partial shade, and temperatures down to -15° to -20°C (5° to -4°F). Added to this, coneflowers put on a good show in their first year. They need replacing or raising from new seed, division, or cuttings every other year. Personally, I find the white-flowering varieties rather too green and insipid, but the jostling heads of the purple varieties – available in shades of red and purple – instantly enliven their setting in late summer.

What could be longer term than the sacred *Ginkgo biloba*, the sole survivor of a group of trees that died out millions of years ago? It is known as the maidenhair tree because of its ferny prehistoric leaves that turn a glorious gold in autumn. The fruit are foul-smelling, so you are better off sticking with a male clone for the garden. The leaves are used in teas and medicines, and favoured for keeping the mind alert and improving circulation. Ginkgo withstands urban pollution and is very resistant to pests and diseases but prefers hot summers.

The chaste tree (*Vitex agnus-castus*) bears elegant aromatic palmate leaves and clusters of fragrant white or lilac flowers up to 15cm (6in) long in autumn. Its seeds were once ground to suppress libido. Today, extracts are used to regulate hormonal functions and promote lactation. The tree requires a warm site with protection from cold, drying winds and good drainage.

Above
At Denmans in Sussex, John Brookes has used the glaucous silvery greens of *Eryngium giganteum* in the foreground with lavender and lady's mantle against the core of purple salvia and yellow of evening primrose and marigolds.

Bulbs

Carefully chosen bulbs, particularly those that are hardy, will thrive in all settings – under grass or as part of a bedding scheme, in shade or full sun, in damp or dry conditions. On top of this, bulbs can give year-round colour and scent. If you are using herbs for underplanting, the winter months are usually rather bare, so for early colour choose crocuses and snowdrops, whose leaves will not damage the later herbs. The prized saffron crocus disappears for much of the year, offering a spring show of leaves and then an autumn display of flowers. The so-called autumn crocus (*Colchicum*) is from a different family and is poisonous – the common name of "naked ladies" perfectly describes the plant's rather long anemic stems. The Madonna lily (*Lilium candidum*) has long elegant stems topped by the whitest of white scented flowers making it a must in any herb collection. The golden-rayed lily (*Lilium auratum*) and the regal lily (*L. regale*) provide scent and height but will need lifting and renewing within five years.

Keeping up appearances

The plant's long-term quality will be enhanced by attending to its cultural needs at every stage. Buy a good specimen, and plant it within good compost as what lies beneath the roots will ensure longevity more than annual mulching. However, weeds can be controlled and moisture conserved by a mulching of gravel or finely shredded bark.

When choosing a small tree as a centrepiece, check at what height you can realistically stop it, and how much space you can afford. Pruning is best done after flowering, or during dormancy, remembering

to always cutting out dead and crossing wood. Evergreens are traditionally pruned in late autumn or mid spring, the latter being advisable with both bay and myrtle. Formal box-hedged gardens should be clipped so that they get one good haircut a year – this can be anytime from early summer to early autumn.

Bergenias and perennial chamomiles need to have dead flowers and leaves removed, and to be lifted and split when they become too crowded. The aftercare of lavenders, santolinas, and thymes should be adjusted to your visual requirements. The frosted flower spikes of lavender make an attractive addition to the winter garden, so prune back to lower buds in spring. If you have a pond or pool with blanket weed, form your lavender prunings into small bundles, and throw them in the water to cure the problem. Santolinas look a mess after flowering, so remove spent branches immediately, then the following spring cut back as you do with lavender. Finally, thymes rapidly become woody, so should be trimmed back immediately after flowering.

As the long-term trees and shrubs establish and cover the soil surface, the instant and short-term herbs will die out, having served their function. You might want to create additional interest by training clematis or honeysuckle around their trunks and through their branches. As the scheme matures, herbs can refresh the appearance of established shrubs and perennials. In summer, sowings of Japanese basil (*Perilla*) provide leaf interest, as does allowing love-in-the-mist to form a light groundcover. Reintroduce clumps of chives planted in uneven numbers or new cushions of thyme. The lasting effect will be a longer display of flowers and foliage interest, and, possibly, scent.

Left
The garden designer Noel Kingsbury has contrasted the shaggy red flowerheads of the bergamot 'Squaw' with the creamy-white plumes of meadowsweet for a sweet-smelling summer profusion.

Right
The Californian designer Topher Delaney has sculpted thyme and paving for a dramatic, modern, geometric effect.

Edible Landscape

Grazing evokes bucolic images of sheep nibbling heather-covered hillsides or cattle up to their knees in rich flowery meadows. Edible landscaping feasts your eyes and stomach, as you graze around shrubberies and flowerbeds enhanced by chard, chives, orache, salad burnet, or any pretty leaf or flower with a bit of zest. Throw off the shackles of creating an ornamental kitchen garden or potager and create a takeaway among paeonies and penstemons. Under whatever name, food plants are rich sources of colour and texture, providing perennial, biennial, annual, and ephemeral interest. Rather than just having roses around the door, consider edible arbours and tunnels, hopefully supporting grapes and passion fruits, beans, peas, and squashes underplanted with cushions of wild strawberries, golden marjoram, and thyme with catch crops of pretty lettuces, chervil, and basil.

At Sooke Harbour House on Vancouver Island, Canada, every plant you see is edible. This is the purist's version of edible landscaping, but the approach I am suggesting is to combine edible and decorative plants for visual effect, with the bonus of a harvest. Edible landscaping can be achieved with one season's good ground preparation; annual maintenance will be reduced, if you include fruit and nuts and a selection of perennial vegetables. If you are undecided about an ornamental area of the garden, experiment for one year with annual vegetables, which will also help to clear and feed the ground. Grand terraces or small patios can be enhanced with containers of clipped citrus or topiary gooseberries underplanted with thymes.

Herbs for edible landscaping

If space allows, plant a sweet bay or certainly have it in a pot for year-round interest. Bay leaves gently infuse their flavour, so do not be afraid to experiment by just dropping a leaf into a wide variety of sweet and savoury dishes. Other herbs to harvest rather than graze are the Provençal herbs such as lavender, hyssop, marjorams, rosemary, sage, thyme, and winter savory.

Previous pages
Masses of chives fill the stepping stones in
one of the potager squares at Villandry
in the Loire Valley in late spring. In former
years sorrel has been used.

Above
Make a virtue of allowing plants to go to
seed. In a pleasing colour scheme, the
sentinel bolted lettuce 'Bijou' combines
with wands of flowering red orache,
asparagus, and the beet 'Bull's Blood'.

Opposite page
In South Africa, the kitchen garden for the
Cellars Hotel in the Cape ensures good
edible pickings are close to hand – the bay
looks as though it has been well used!

Horseradish is rarely well grown, because few people bother to lift
and transplant it early in the season. The long, stick-like roots should
be lifted either in autumn or spring, cut into 8cm (3in) lengths, and
replanted in rich soil – this helps to harvest better-tasting roots.
Those with variegated foliage sit ornamentally among a wide
selection of herbaceous perennials that like rich soil.

Grazing for pleasure depends on the time of the year, and late spring
and summer seasons are certainly best; the summer may fade but the
herbs become increasingly strong – not bitter but mouth drying and
medicinal. If you like the taste of onions, then nibbling chives will be
a treat, the new firm tips or the freshly formed florets are equally
delicious. For an aniseed flavour, the young seed heads of sweet cicely
in late spring taste just like aniseed balls; later in the year the yellow
umbels of fennel are instantly reviving. Sorrel has a wonderful acidic
freshness; the large-leaved French variety looks good but for flavour and
tidiness I prefer the buckler-leaved sorrel, especially its silver form.

Cool refreshing mint is a culinary gem, but do not let its
invasiveness in the garden intimidate you. Simply lift the mint every
other year, cut it back to fresh young runners, and throw away old
rootstocks. Then, settle back to enjoy white, yellow, and purple
variegations, a heavenly mint scent, and grazing rights.

When planning edible landscaping with vegetables as well as herbs
you need to follow the basic crop rotation – potatoes, roots, legumes,
and brassicas. Many of the ornamental vegetables were originally
mentioned in herbals: statuesque globe artichokes and cardoons provide
height, as do hops or runner beans trained up tripods. Asparagus peas

need harvesting every day but they will flower throughout the summer, with deep-red flowers nestling in grey-green foliage followed by tiny frilled peas that look as though they are wearing a party dress.

Wise sages

The sage was introduced by the Romans, who rightly advised never to cut it with an iron blade, as iron salts react with chemicals in sage. Such are the medicinal properties of sage that a wealth of folklore has grown up around it – you could try eating it every day in May for eternal life, rubbing it onto your gums for healthy teeth, or applying it to the roots of your hair as a conditioner. The common green sage (*Salvia officinalis*) and the purple-leaved sages (*S. o.* Purpurascens Group) make decorative and aromatic additions to any garden.

Herbalists today use them as anti-inflammatories, astringents, antiseptics, and to relax spasms. Drinking sage tea is also supposed to suppress perspiration and stop lactation. What is more, these sages improve liver function and digestion as well as being anti-depressants. However, all this assumes eating sane quantities, because sage contains a camphoraceous oil, of which 50 percent is thujone; taken in excess it can be hallucinogenic, addictive, and toxic. The lavender sage (*S. lavandulifolia*) has no thujone and also has digestive and medicinal properties; it is widely used for dried sage but I prefer the taste of the green and purple forms. The salvia family includes some beautiful, scented, tender plants such as the pineapple sage, whose bright red flowers appear in late summer, and whose almost succulent leaves exude a pineapple scent.

Herbs, annual but easy

Remember the principles of seed-sowing: a seed should never be sown deeper than its own size, and newly dug ground should be raked and firmed, not compacted. Water the surface until thoroughly moistened, scatter the seeds, and cover them with dry compost or soil. This will prevent drying breezes from penetrating the topsoil.

Summer savory can be closely sown to provide a green carpet with dots of pale pink flowers that stand until autumn. Salad rocket and wild rocket come under a variety of names: arugula, roquette, ruchètta or ruca, often mistranslated as rue. Rocket leaves have a nutty flavour and the creamy yellow flowers a nutty fragrance. Salad rocket seems to grow much better earlier and later in the year, when the days are either lengthening or shortening. Throughout spring and summer scatter sow coriander, chervil, or dill for a feathery effect and a range of tastes.

Basils are easy to germinate but hard to grow on. Treat them like a tender annual, sowing them only when the days and nights have really warmed up and there is absolutely no fear of frost. Provide good, rich, well-drained soil, so that hopefully the basil sits in sun-warmed dry soil, as the temperatures drop at night; a south-facing wall or path are ideal sites. Basils offer as much colour as tender exotics – deep purple leaves that are silky smooth or crinkled, and large or small, with aniseed, cinnamon, and scented flavours. Holy basil maintains a compact form with soft, pale green leaves and pink flowers. The more tender lemon basil, with a winning combination of lemon and basil flavours, also has pale green leaves. And don't forget the green range of sweet and bush basils, the cook's friends: the sweet Genovese is excellent; the lettuce-leaved is the answer to a pesto-maker's prayer; and the bush-type fine-leaved and Greek basils thrive in terracotta pots. Water them when the compost is dry and in the morning. Not only are tomatoes and basil good culinary partners but the gross-feeding tomato leaves the basil half starved and able to thrive!

Flowers

Obvious herb flowers such as chives, fennel, and nasturtiums are just the starters in the edible-flower stakes. The pale lemon day lilies (*Hemerocallis*) are crunchy, while the petals of dark roses can be nibbled as you pass by, harvested for traditional recipes, notably jams and jellies, or scattered over chocolate cakes or fresh fruit salads.

It's not too late to sow

Although most annuals are sown in spring, later summer sowings can provide fresh, soft offerings right up to the first frosts. They will not mature or give the bumper crops that you get from seeds sown earlier but they are an edible bonus. Do remember that a seed first produces an adventitious root before its seedling leaves, so late sowings will benefit from a richer compost to boost their start. An advantage of late sowings is that they are best done direct into the soil or final containers. Basil, chervil, coriander, dill, and salad rocket are personal favourites – they will grow larger than sprouted seeds but smaller and softer than herbs sown earlier. In Atlanta, Georgia, I was served a zesty, vitamin-boosting "microsalad", which consisted of a selection of herb seeds newly sprouted and harvested when barely 2cm (¾in) tall.

Opposite page left
The American Kitchen Garden at Frelinghuysen Arboretum in New Jersey uses a forest of poles to allow climbing vegetables to tower over herb underplantings.

Opposite page right
A compact arrangement of lettuces 'Leprachaun' and 'Aruba' combine with the fat hens *Chenopodium giganteum* and *C.capitatum* in The Cooks Garden at Ryton Organic Gardens, Warwickshire.

Below
This is a close-up of the pinky red-splashed centres of *Chenopodium capitatum*, an ornamental edible that needs to be eaten young.

Freestyle

One of the hardest effects to achieve when designing and planting up a new area is the look of careless rapture. Freestyle gardening gets you away from the drawing board and seed catalogues to work with what thrives in your soil. Conversely, those of us who have lived with the same garden for decades have to beware of letting nature do the work unmonitored. The marvellous billowing effect of a sea of lavender, cotton lavender, or catmint under and around roses and shrubs needs to be kept in check with an annual hard prune to maintain maximum leaf and flower and minimum dead wood. Golden marjoram is a herald of spring renewal, its cushions of gold and variegated gold gradually taking a back seat as the light green leaves provide a foil and low windbreak for later plants and early sowings. Sweet woodruff offers a gentle mantle of green, dotted with white starry spring flowers, under the dappled shade of small trees and shrubs. The freestyle look is enhanced by herbs and wild flowers left to flower and set seeds, which drop to the ground around them, forming natural drifts.

Sloping off

The best way to see the planted slopes at the Nunobiki Herb Garden in Kobe, Japan, is to take the cable car on the way up, then to walk alongside them on the way down. The hairpin route is decorated with a massed bedding display, with herbs, including heartsease, a kitchen garden with the brightest calendula marigolds I have ever seen, then down through a veritable field of lavender, a wild flower garden, a blue garden, a fragrance garden, and finally the dramatic "Waterfall Rest". At one point the path narrows to a long series of steps edged with an abundance of feverfew and poppies, the white daisies jostling with the bright red flowers. The sage family includes an enormous selection of tender salvias with red, purple, pink, yellow, and bicoloured flowers set against tender foliage in hues of green and purple. At Nunobiki they are woven into a groundcover display from the path to the tree line. Another bank has a massed planting of dwarf sunflowers.

Rather than just grassing a natural slope, check its aspect and plant it up. Planting introduces movement, especially on south- and west-facing slopes, which are ideal for sun-loving herbs with long flower stalks such as lavender and catmint. At the Hexham Walled Garden in Northumberland, Susie White has planted her National Collection of Thymes the length of a bank, creating a colourful display. To prevent them becoming woody, she cuts them back to within 0.6cm (¼in) of new growth immediately after flowering. A more modest massed planting of lemon thyme may not be as visually effective but it will be more ruggedly naturalistic. At Buscot Park in Oxfordshire a sunken area has been created and paved for potted citrus, with the surrounding banks planted with golden variegated periwinkle. The periwinkles have an ancient and powerful medicinal history but they are safe to handle and grow; they are very hardy and almost evergreen. On the north bank of our hawthorn hedge, the creeping variegated comfrey (*Symphytum grandiflora*) has colonized and naturalized but still allows snowdrops and daffodils to push through in late winter and spring. The blue-flowered comfrey (*S. caucasicum*) is an alternative groundcover.

Edwardian gardeners such as Gertrude Jekyll strongly advised terracing slopes with steps and low retaining walls for flowerbeds. Even in an area of naturally occurring stone or flint this can be an expensive proposition – unless you create the hard landscaping yourself – but with the introduction of linear plant colour and texture the effect is gracious. Walls also create a microclimate, so are ideal for borderline hardy herbs and plants, and for enhancing scent.

On the flat

Roof gardens and landscapes were transformed by the 20th-century Brazilian garden designer, Roberto Burle Marx. South American gardens had hitherto been dictated by old-fashioned European formal designs, but Burle Marx broke the mould by realizing the potential of Brazil's exuberant native flora. The way he expresses the relationship between architecture and design as "beauty of form allied to function; interrelation of volumes, forms, colors; aesthetics in relation to social and psychological ends" may sound far from freestyle, but its practice is dramatic, sculpting a flat surface into swathes of interest.

Areas of level ground are divided into shapes, with each shape having just one plant variety. The plants can run harmoniously alongside one another or in direct contrast. If you are a Burle Marx enthusiast, you could choose tropical-looking plants such as cannas, pampas grass, and *Verbena bonariensis* with exotic-looking herbs such as the silver buckler-leaved sorrel, mullein, euphorbia, and elecampane. For architectural contrast, use spires of black cohosh or the luminous blue of eryngiums such as 'Miss Wilmott's Ghost', separated by the almost evergreen bergenia and ultra-hardy lady's mantle. Supplement with annual plantings of the purple-leaved Japanese basil or self-set love-in-a-mist under which you could have winter and spring bulbs.

One of the hardiest shade lovers to brighten up spring plantings is lungwort (*Pulmonaria* spp.), named because its white-spotted leaves look like a lung. In Europe it was believed that drops of the Virgin's milk or her tears had fallen onto the leaves, hence its other name of Virgin Mary's milkdrops. Here, in Suffolk, it is also known as soldiers and sailors because of the blue and pink flowers. There are some very pretty modern cultivars such as the dark blue-flowered and elegantly spotted 'Beth Chatto' and the later flowering 'Mawson's Blue'.

Self-starters

Many perennial, biennial, and annual herbs self-seed but unlike cuttings you will not get an exact replica of the parent herb. The early leaves of angelica are excellent in salads, and the ferny fronds of sweet cicely counteract the oxalic acid in rhubarb. When the spring leaves have been harvested, allow them to flower and go to seed – both germinate best from fresh seed. The seedlings are easy to identify and will establish in any ground, gravel, or grass. Both herbs provide a dramatic backdrop but need plenty of space. Poppy, sorrel, and lady's mantle rapidly become thugs, so, as the flowers fade, cut back to a few flowerheads to set seed. Beware of edible thugs such as dandelions, whose "clocks" blow on the wind or the burdock's sticky "pin cushions".

Salad rocket and chervil will self-seed once or twice during the year; gently weed around the parent plant so that the seeds can fall directly into soil. Weather permitting, fresh pickings can be available nine months of the year. In warmer climates, the seed of coriander or cilantro will survive in the ground over winter, germinating to give early pickings. Hyssop, lavender, marjoram, and thyme self-seed generously but the seedlings tend to vary from the parent plant.

If you have space, buy a male and female sweet bay – the mimosa-like blossoms on the female are a scented joy in late spring, followed by black berries, which drop in late autumn.

Opposite page
A native of North America, the butterfly weed (*Asclepias tuberosa*) will naturalize on an open sunny site, its summer flowers attracting hummingbirds and butterflies.

Below
In the naturalized Arts and Crafts-inspired woodlands in Vann, in Surrey, the white-flowering Ramsons garlic has colonized with bluebells and ferns.

Evening Gardens

On warm evenings what could be nicer than a relaxing drink or supper under the skies? Somehow you forget all about the chores that await you inside. With judicious planting you can enhance dusk and darkness with scented luminiscence – start by looking for plants with "moon" or "white" in their names. Many evening and night plants are trying to attract pollinating moths and insects with their scent and colour, the result of which is an equal draw for us.

Summer evenings lengthen the further you are from the equator, so by midsummer, in some zones, darkness may not fall until after ten o'clock at night. These long, hopefully sunny, days help flowers and herbs to catch up with their equivalents in warmer zones. It is worth noting this when you are travelling, as many gardens reach their zenith late in the summer.

Night sight

In the mid-19th century a Bohemian scientist, Johannes Evangelista Purkinje, amongst other anatomical discoveries, described the "Purkinje phenomenon". He noted that only the cones in our eyes distinguish colour, while the rods within the periphery of the retina are colour-blind, so see only in black and white. The rest of the eye can see blue and yellow, while the centre is restricted to red and green. Purkinje discovered that in dim light the ability to see red and green disappears, leaving our vision restricted to blue and yellow plus black, white, and shades of grey. As the light fades so do its warm yellows but the white light remains clear, creating a black sky punctured with twinkling stars and moonlight. This is because the cones cease to function, leaving the rods to record in black and white. In short, borders filled with daytime, fiery red flowers and interesting green leaves are evening bores. Conversely, purples and mauves draw the eye at dusk, a mound of purple sage will replace what flowering aubretia has provided earlier. Catmint (*Nepeta* spp.) is featured frequently in this book and yet again joins the evening chorus.

Previous pages
At Penns in the Rocks in Sussex the setting sun gives a golden glow to the lavender and clipped box. Note how the white bench and silver santolina retain their brightness.

Above
In this design Bunny Guinness has enhanced the luminiscent qualities of the purple sage by backing it with a pale mauve trellis.

Opposite page above
Night-scented stock is perfectly named; this variety, *Matthiola longipetala* ssp. *bicornis*, has exceptionally showy flowers.

Opposite page below
The golden yellows opposite the blue hydrangea draw the eye to the standing stone and then along the curving path at The Garden House, Buckland Monochorum in Devon.

A delightful example has been created at West Green, in Hampshire, where a staggered line of catmint fronts the splashed white variegated *Pelargonium* 'Moonglow' and the delicate pinky-white umbels of coriander. This makes a virtue of coriander's uncontrollable desire to flower rather than produce leaves, with the bonus that you can then harvest the seeds later.

Crepuscular aspect

The plan on pp.68–9 suggests a scheme for an evening garden. Instead of a brick wall you could erect a fence or, alternatively, a trellis to catch the setting sun and the day's warmth. In France you frequently see trellis used to create *trompe l'oeil* in the most mundane situations. For the evening garden, pale paint colours such as light blue or dove grey will transform the cheapest trellis. The paving could be brick, stone, or fine gravel – ideally choose creams, whites, or greys to maintain a visual effect that is pale and luminescent.

The climbers are trained up poles and around the framework, not across it; if you are planning to use the arbour during the day you might train the vines across to provide shade but in the evening you want to enjoy the stars and moonlight. The elegant flowers, leaves, and twining habit of wisteria make it a perfect candidate for training over wood, iron, or stone. The pendulous purple racemes of the Japanese wisteria (*Wisteria floribunda*) can be 60cm (24in) long and will contrast with the smaller white flowers of the Chinese wisteria (*W. sinensis* 'Alba') in early summer; the secondary flowering is less spectacular but the pinnate leaves are very attractive. The glaucous-leaved *Vitis vinifera* 'Incana' will gleam in the moonlight, contrasting with the dark purple-leaved *V. v.* 'Purpurascens'. After a good summer the leaves of the latter should be a triumph. The bonus of planting vines is that you might get a crop of grapes as well.

If you have space and a strong-enough framework, maximize the effect by weaving in some other climbers. The potato vine (*Solanum jasminoides*) has, as its names suggests, starry flowers like white jasmine; it climbs better than the common jasmine but does not have the scent. Be warned: the Victorian rose 'Madame Alfred Carrière' is

very vigorous but will grow on a north wall or in dappled shade and has masses of the palest pink, lightly-scented flowers. No evening garden would be complete without the annual addition of the moonflower (*Ipomea alba*), whose white flowers are so dense that the leaves are almost invisible.

In the strictest sense phormium is more of a herb than yucca; both provide dramatic sword-shaped leaves and extraordinarily tall flower spikes. However, my choice is influenced by Henry Bright, who in 1901 wrote of his experiences in *A Year in a Lancashire Garden*. Sadly, he had failed to get his yucca to send "pale jets of blossom, like fountains, towards the sky...", but then saw several by moonlight in Shropshire. Bright quotes the 19th-century American writer, Margaret Fuller: "This flower was made for the moon as the Heliotrope is for the sun...", and adds from his own experience, "The stalk pierced the air like a spear; all the bells had erected themselves around it in most graceful array with petals more transparent than silver, and of softer light than the diamond. Their edges were clearly but not sharply defined – they seemed fringed by most delicate gossamer, and the plant might claim, with pride, its distinctive epithet of filamentosa". If that has not convinced you, nothing will. The flowering spikes can reach 4.5m (15ft). The variegated leaves of *Y. gloriosa* grow up to 60cm (24in) long, and its flowering spikes up to 2.4m (8ft) long. The scene is set: now you need scent and more colour.

The planting is focused on the four corners, so that you can come and go with ease and yet have a sense of private enclosure. The bold architectural lines of the yuccas need skirting plants and echoing

N

Evening Garden Plan

Plant list

Common names
1 Large-flowered yarrow
2 Peruvian lily
3 Variegated borage
4 White-flowering foxglove
5 Variegated strawberry
6 Summer hyacinth
7 Dame's rocket
8 Dwarf hyssop
9 Moonflower
10 Variegated Juno iris
11 *Lavandula allardii*
12 Pineapple mint
13 Variegated applemint
14 Flowering tobacco
15 Love-in-a-mist
16 Vesper iris
17 White-flowering
    perennial phlox
18 *Rosa* 'Madame
    Alfred Carrière'
19 Purple sage
20 Cotton lavender
     'Lemon Queen'
21 Double-flowering soapwort
22 Potato vine
23 Woolly thyme
24 Variegated periwinkle
25 Glaucous-leaved vine
26 Purple-leaved vine
27 Japanese wisteria
28 White-flowering Chinese
    wisteria
29 Spoonleaf yucca
30 Variegated palm lily

flowers. Combine herbs such as variegated mints and periwinkle with the luminiscent, pale, shaggy pink flowers of the soapworts. You can repeat this less dramatically with a variegated borage, whose blue, star-like flowers contrast attractively with its yellow variegated leaves, or with the pretty white-flowering form. There is also the bonus of picking the flowers and leaves to float in your white wine, Pimms, or gin and tonic, while sampling the nearby sweet fruits of the more ornamental variegated strawberry (*Fragaria* x *ananassa variegata*).

The variegated Juno iris provides sustained interest with its white-variegated leaves and pale purple flowers. The flowers of the vesper iris (*Pardanthopsis dichotoma*) are not much to look at but have a sweet fragrance, so drift them through the plantings, so that their scent wafts on the evening air. On a smaller scale, night-scented stock should be liberally sown around the plantings. The Latin name for dame's violet – *Hesperis matronalis* – is a corruption of vesper or evening; free-flowering in white and mauve forms, it is an easy and invaluable herbal addition. The yellow-green or white flowers of the flowering tobacco (*Nicotiana alata*) will make a statement and release a heady perfume.

Yarrow, whose leaves staunched the blood of Achilles, have a good range of ornamental relations. *Achillea grandifolia* bears flat white corymbs that create a visual layer in the planting. The late-summer scent of the Peruvian lily (*Gladiolus callianthus*) reminds me of the smell of suntan oil. Other white-flowering choices include foxgloves; summer hyacinths (*Galtonia* spp.), which look more like oversized lilies of the valley; the traditional but unbeatable panicles of phlox; and the white form of love-in-a-mist gently self-seeding a flowery web.

Four further herbs can provide layers of discreet tone and aromatic scent. For hedging or as individual plants, I would recommend the large, free-flowering lavender *Lavandula* x *allardii* and the pale yellow pompom flowers of the cotton lavender *Santolina chamaecyparissus* 'Lemon Queen'. The rock hyssop forms a spiky aromatic cushion with fuller purple flowers than the taller form, and you can throw it on the barbecue or use it in fruit syrups. Let the woolly thyme carpet and colonize the dry edges of soil and paving; it is no good for cooking but a delight to look at and touch.

Frosty features

Unless you have good heaters you will probably not be sitting outside in the cold months, but the winter garden offers its own visual delights. A moonlight walk on a frosty night is enhanced by formal plantings; it is the magic of Philippa Pearce's novel *Tom's Midnight Garden*, peopled by clipped evergreens such as yew and box to which you can add bay and myrtle. We have no street lights, so on a moonlit winter evening I switch off the lights indoors and look out through a tiny window on the stairs onto the unclipped silvery flowerheads of golden marjoram, hedges of box and *Euonymus japonicus*, golden bay backed with sweet bay, and the patterned background of deciduous trees.

When you look at your garden in the moonlight you are presented with a black-and-white image that will help you to review the overall design. Do the flower spires provide effective architectural accents? Do the curvaceous leaves overlap to give texture and tone? Finally, and most importantly as far as this book is concerned, are the herbs making a good contribution?

Herb Boundaries

Box, yew, and hawthorn provide traditional impenetrable hedges with important medicinal uses. Each hedging variety makes a subtle statement about its planter's taste: box is inextricably associated with kitchen gardens and Victorian cottage gardens; clipped yew provides an immaculate dark backdrop, while its golden variety can play a decorative solo role as it catches the morning and evening sun; hawthorn is the country hedge that in Britain stout lines narrow lanes and old gardens, a haven for birds and other wildlife.

The Red Garden at Hidcote Manor in Gloucestershire is famed for its "tapestry" hedge of copper beech, yew, and Scottish flame flower, and I have used the same idea in a variety of combinations. The round, glossy leaves of box create a mosaic pattern when trimmed hard against the needle sprays of yew, while the hawthorn opens up the texture, providing changing hues, flowers, and fruit. Only the hawthorn yields a realistic medicinal harvest – the country name for the young leaves is "bread and cheese", and the unexciting flavour of the haws does not diminish their value to herbalists as a warming herb that improves peripheral circulation.

It is essential that the hedge is kept well trimmed. If you wait until early summer you can reduce the number of times you need to take out the shears, because the earlier you start, the more you'll encourage the hedge to grow. In wet summers even so-called slow-growers rapidly put out new shoots, so allow a little initial untidiness.

Decorative hedging
One of the main purposes of a hedge is to demarcate boundary changes, and for this there are a number of herbs that will make a softer and scented alternative to the lower box hedges that are so frequently used. Lavender and catmint are good choices, and their grey-green and silver leaves offset by myriad purple spikes personify summer gardens. Both benefit from a thoroughly good haircut each year so take them back to the lowest two or three buds. If it has been

Previous pages
At Penshurst Place in Sussex, the flag garden formed out of lavender hedges and infilled with pink roses flies brightly within its boundaries.

Above
The rose garden at Helmingham Hall in Suffolk has mixed plantings elegantly outlined with clipped hyssop hedging.

Opposite page
Under blue skies and Phoenix palms a cotton lavender-lined path leads up to and around the handsome agave at Cotijo Papudo in Spain.

a dry summer, leave the flowerheads as a winter architectural feature and cut back in mid-spring. A wet summer, however, encourages floppy flower heads that just end up as a soggy mass in winter. Take lavender cuttings after four years with a view to replanting. When you lift the old lavender hedge, dig over the ground and incorporate new fibrous compost. Catmints are best lifted and split after about five years. Carol Klein suggests underplanting with autumn crocus (*Colchicum*), which neatly engulfs their anemic stems, and subtly echoes their flowers in hues of pink, mauve or white.

Hyssops are used less frequently for hedging, probably because they are freer in their outline than lavender or catmint. In my design for the Tudor knot garden at Yalding Organic Gardens in Kent, I wove hyssops with germander, and the gardeners let them flower each summer, bringing a flush of pink and blue to the design. The two knots were originally enclosed by a clipped rosemary hedge but the heavy clay and cold Kent winters sounded the death knell for many of them, leaving a very gappy effect, so we replanted with box. However, if you live near the coast, rosemary, the "rose of the sea", will thrive where other plants fail. At Helmingham Hall in Suffolk hyssop is alternated with lavender in the scented garden, while at nearby Hintlesham Hall Beth Chatto used the dwarf or rock hyssop (*Hyssopus aristatus*) as an edging to one of the culinary herb beds. Hyssops are very free seeders – the pink flowerers are likely also to produce purple flowers, while the white and blue are interchangeable. Cut back flowering branches in autumn to prevent winter windrock and then cut back to the lowest buds in late spring to prevent a woody mess.

With their silver or green ferny foliage and mass of button flowers, the cotton lavenders (*Santolina* spp.) are versatile plants, useful for low hedging or in single or massed plantings. The origin of their name *sanctum linum*, or holy flax, provides a clue to their pleasant sharp scent and delicate leaves. The common varieties, reaching a height and spread of about 50cm (19in), are strains of *Santolina chamaecyparissus* and include: 'Lambrook Silver' with tinted silver leaves; 'Lemon Queen' with a mass of pale lemon flowers; and the more compact 'Pretty Carol'. My personal favourite is *S. pinnata* ssp. *neapolitana* which can reach a size of 70cm (30in) and has very open growth with fronded leaves and a mass of pale yellow pompom flowers. Good green-leaved varieties include the rosemary-leaved santolina with bright yellow flowers. The varieties grow well together, especially in contrasting blocks as a stepping-stone boundary. Good maintenance can give you almost year-round good looks. When you grow santolinas you will notice that although the branches become woody, there are invariably healthy buds in the centre of the shrub. If you prune back to these buds you will maintain the plant in better shape.

Cushion edging

Golden marjorams (*Origanum vulgare* 'Aureum') can be planted at almost any time of the year – although not, as you would expect, during periods of hard frost or summer drought – and they will settle rapidly to provide soft-scented edgings in a matter of weeks. In a small area the crinkled leaves of *O. v.* 'Aureum Crispum' and 'Thumble's Variety' provide added interest, opening the season with bright gold

leaves that fade to a golden green. There are also golden and silver variegated forms; the golden varieties, including 'Gold Tip' are hardier than silver forms such as 'Well-Sweep', which are better treated as single specimens. Marjorams are so easy to grow, split, and replant that they are ideal plants to tease into curvaceous and audacious lines running in and around your plot. As with lavenders and catmint, if you have had a good hot summer consider leaving the flowerheads for winter architectural interest. Whether you have cut them back or not, after rain and on sunny winter days they will exude a delicious scent.

Thymes come in so many forms that it is worth being aware that the softer the leaf the less hardy and also shorter lived the thyme will be. The common, lemon, and orange thymes are all longer lived and extremely hardy in well-drained, sunny positions. The creeping thymes will happily colonize gravel and the cracks and crevices of paths, but it is best to start them off in earth at the edge of gravel or paths and leave them to establish. At Sissinghurst in Kent, the "Persian Carpet" is a central feature in a path, an idea that you might want to replicate in your garden by copying the pattern of a rug or carpet on the ground and then selecting thymes to match the design.

Keeping out intruders

If you need to make your boundaries rabbit-proof, the taller lavenders and santolinas will mask low fencing; voracious rabbits will eat lavender but tend to leave the santolinas alone. Wormwood (*Artemisia absinthium*) deters many animals, so you could plant drifts of it along the fence. Finally, avoid growing nepeta if you want to keep cats away.

Below
At Essebourne Manor, Hampshire, thyme and catmint create inner boundaries that nestle around a seat without excluding the landscape beyond.

Opposite page
The fountain under the metal archway at Hitcham House in Suffolk is engulfed by a tidal wave of the magnificent catmint *Nepeta* x *faassenii* 'Six Hills Giant'.

Texture & Tone

Herbs offer hues of green, purple, gold, and silver; a diverse selection of shapes ranging from the toweringly statuesque to creeping mats; and textures that are downy, smooth, bristly, dissected, or succulent. Classic formal designs are created using clipped hedging, topiary, and pleached trees in geometric symmetry, for which bay, myrtle, and box are ideal. Lose the vanishing point by crossing mounds of herbs and other herbaceous plants that lead the eye from side to side in a fashion that has inspired Japanese art and gardens for centuries. Both approaches can be applied to either distant or close-up appreciation of individual plantings.

Look and touch

Herbs offer wonderful leaf textures – woolly, crinkled, feathery, and grassy leaves, arranged in clumps, mounds, and spires. Most herb flowers are discreet but when massed in umbels, bells, or balls they can ring the changes in a border's progression, not forgetting the daisies, spikes, and seedheads that they can also contribute.

Herbs with dramatic spikes tower out of their surroundings, providing texture and tone, and, for those who like a good story, folklore and mystery. From its deadly poisonous seeds rises the castor-oil plant (*Ricinus communis*), with great, red-edged palmate leaves and vivid red panicles soaring to heights of up to 2m (6½ft). The velvety-leaved mullein (*Verbascum* spp.) has tapering yellow spires of flowers nestled in white downy stems, which gleam in the moonlight, marching like triffids when given free rein across the garden. They are easy to weed out and best randomly planted. The erect resinous stems were formerly dipped in tallow and used as poor man's candles and, when picked, the leaves can be used to store ripe figs. The rightly named *V. olympicum* forms a silver-white rosette up to 1m (3ft) across before forming a majestic white-stemmed candelabra up to 1.8m (6ft) high. There are cultivars as short as 60cm (24in) and flowers ranging from shades of white and yellow to buff pink and purple.

Yuccas and phormiums will both create substantial architectural clumps. Apart from their broad flat leaves, yuccas send up pale jets of blossom, like fountains reaching over 2m (6½) towards the sky. Phormiums, commonly known as New Zealand flax, are fit for both use and delight: their fibres were once widely used in the textile trade. The broad-bladed leaves come in a range of colours and variegations. Phormiums are wind tolerant, so put them to good use and enjoy the sound as they filter the breeze. The plum-coloured flowering stem of *P. tenax* offers a pleasing contrast to the fans of foliage and can reach a height of 5m (16ft).

If you like the linear quality that sword-leaved plants such as yucca and phormium provide, continue the theme with irises from the willowly Tall Bearded varieties down to the edging *Iris pumila* and scented *I. reticulata*, which are a late-spring delight. Contrast them with slimline ornamental grasses (you are spoilt for choice) as well as grassy herbs, for example, chives. The Chinese or garlic chives have broader leaf spikes, and their white flowers are more ornamental, and just as delicious, forming just once in late summer.

The globular mauve-pink flowers of common chives sit atop grass-like leaves. As soon as chives have finished flowering, cut them back to the base so that you keep the fresh young shoots coming. Ramsons garlic naturalizes with brio in damp grassland and deciduous shade, its long, rounded clusters of white, star-like flowers are borne above the foliage in late spring and early summer. Whether sword, spear, wand, or spike, the visual impact of these plants will benefit from being set alongside gentle mounds and hummocks.

What you may lack in ground space can be compensated by taking the pictorial composition into the sky. Statuesque teasels (*Dipsacus fullonum*) are more suitable for the wild garden, and the haze of mauve flowers around the spiky head form seedheads that will be much appreciated by goldfinches. Fennels, especially the bronze variety (*Foeniculum vulgare* 'Purpureum'), perform several textural tasks in the garden. In spring the almost black foliage creates a ferny sea around bulbs and other spring flowers. As the days lengthen, so do the stems, rising to a height of 1.5m (5ft), and topped with delicate yellow umbels, which contrast with the fading bronze foliage and taste delicious in fruit salads. Their gaunt yet filigree appearance elegantly lightens the back of a summer border.

For instant tone, you can sow purple, green, and golden oraches (*Atriplex hortensis*) to provide wands of colour among other plantings, giving a spot effect. They are edible when young but decidedly chewy and dry once they head upwards to 1–2m (3–6½ft).

The safest, best-tried use of herbs is as a sub-shrub mound, gently rounding a design as it draws the eye away or attempts to build up height with taller shrubs. The mounds can be tended to suit your style: clipped oriental, sculptural globes, or flowering, soft curves. Successful co-plantings include the spreading mounds of sage, especially the purple-leaved variety, punctuated with ornamental alliums. They are low maintenance, so you will have nothing to do apart from occasional weeding for at least five years. *Ruta graveolens* 'Jackman's Blue' has a glorious blue-grey leaf, which inspired the suit of clubs in playing cards. Use the foliage to good effect around roses and figs. It is also an insect repellent, but take care when handling it on sunny days, as the leaves can give you spectacular blisters. The white variegated form is especially attractive, but the yellow flowers have little to offer, and in a small garden you might choose to keep it lightly clipped. In spring be ruthless in taking the plant back to the second or third buds.

Southernwood (*Artemisia abrotanum*) has tough, resilient, silver-green feathery foliage. The plant will attain a height of 1m (3ft) but it is better kept annually cut back. It shows excellently against a

Above
A curtain of wisteria and vines is lifted to
reveal the box hedging softened by wild
planting that lines the path of rough gravel.
The *Lychnis chalcedonica* provides spots
of colour under the fruit trees.

Right
Paving and grass combine to create a
clean modernist effect. The geometric
arrangement is softened by the tidal
wave of nepeta.

backdrop of clipped yew or foreground of clipped box. In the same genus as the wormwoods, it reputedly has aphrodisiac qualities and is a stimulant to hair growth!

If you have grass paths or beds surrounding a lawn you will need to keep the mounds within the bounds of the bed – it is deeply disheartening cutting grass under summer-spreading mounds and edgers. If you have gravel, paving, or brick paths then soften their look by allowing plants to tumble over the edges; many plants benefit from the good drainage as well. Choose plants for their visual appeal, such as unusual leaves or architectural shape. Almost indestructible and bejewelled with dew on most mornings is *Alchemilla mollis*. The soft velvety leaves inspired the common name lady's mantle, and its textured mounds cloak the ground in almost any conditions. The haze of pale yellow flowers typifies voluptuous summer planting. In dry sunny conditions the creamy and pale green hues can be used in harmony with lamb's ears (*Stachys byzantina*), whose thick, woolly, grey leaves grow up to 10cm (4in) long.

Closely related to *Stachys* are the horehounds: the white woolly *Marrubium vulgare*, *Ballota frutescens*, and *B. nigra*, the first and last being medicinal herbs. The first is the smaller, with pleasing downy nettle-like leaves and flowers that grow in whorls up the stem; the stems last well into winter and look delightful coated in frost. The rounded grey-green woolly leaves of *B. frutescens* sit attractively on this branching sub-shrub. If you have a warm sheltered spot you might try the woolly lavender (*Lavandula lanata*), or keep it in a pot – a movable feast in and out of the garden.

Japanese basil (*Perilla*) is marginally easier to grow than true basil (*Ocimum*) and has gorgeous crinkly leaves that are deep purple, almost black, or like clear green crepe paper. You will need good drainage and sun, and the willpower to resist eating too much until the basil is established. The deep purple brings a grotto-like quality to a planting as it draws the eye deep into the complex leaf detail. The leaf colour complements pink flowers especially well.

Two other annual herbs that benefit from being allowed to self-seed set a floriferous tone: the poppy (pink and red *Papaver somniferum*) and love-in-a-mist (*Nigella damascena*) recalls the veiled Scheherazade in the romantic tale, tirelessly spinning her tales while weaving her fine foliage and pale blue flowers in gentle waves. Both plants have the secondary value of ornamental seedheads for the house or garden.

The cracks and crevices of paved and brick paths or gravel provide ideal conditions for creeping thymes or, in moist shade, Corsican mint. *Thymus lanunginosus* must be dry and sunny to produce its downy blanket, through which the mauvy-pink thyme flowers provide a soft, well-established look to a garden. It is better to plant creepers in the soil at the path's margins, rather than trying to push rootlets into harsh corners – they will then venture a root hold in the cracks, doing less damage to themselves.

Texture and tone in a garden should invite you not just to look but also to touch: to run your hands over clipped mounds or through open branches and draw your face into the blooms to savour their scent. If the summer and autumn are dry, leave as many herb flowerheads as possible to provide winter architectural interest and, in the case of origanums and balms, invigorate scent after frosts or rain.

Design Drama

The many qualities that herbs have to offer have been well rehearsed and previewed – now for their performance. Ideas need to evolve, so mistakes are part of transforming a design into a successful garden with herbs. Whatever size your plot, begin by assessing the site: is it warm and sheltered, in full sun or shade, exposed to winds or in a frost pocket?

What aspect will the plants have? On a sunny day watch where the light falls: a garden with morning sun will be east facing; almost day long, south facing; with afternoon and setting sun, west facing; and with little sunlight, a northerly aspect. A sunny site is one enjoying seven hours or more sunshine in the summer, so it will either be west or south facing. A shady bed needs no more than four hours sunshine a day, so it can be east or north facing. Remember that the shade from trees and plants is preferable to the blanket shade of buildings. Determine the soil pH. Most herbs prefer neutral to alkaline conditions: neutral is 6.5–7.5, acidic below, and alkaline above. A good clue will be what is growing around you – rhododendrons and heathers thrive on lower pHs, and berberis and brassicas on alkaline soils.

Herbs as stars

Very few herbs come into the "star" category apart from beautifully clipped topiary, which is discussed in Shaping Up (*see pp.130-35*). However, there is a good selection with statuesque qualities, and many with winning flowers. The Scottish thistle, teasel, mullein, and clary sage are tall and stately; all self-seed enthusiastically but their seedlings are recognizable and can be controlled by autumn and spring hand weeding. Two North American native herbs, culver's root and bugbane, may not sound inviting but they have great spires of white flowers. Culver's root (*Veronicastrum virginicum*), also known as bowman's root or tall speedwell, has a mass of small, snapdragon-like flowers and thrives in rich, moist, lightly shaded ground. Bugbane (*Cimicifuga racemosa*), with white, wand-like flowers, prefers an acidic soil.

Previous pages
The clipped box hedges hold back the
chorus line of winter savory and mint
but your attention is drawn to the
waving flower spikes of fat hen.

Above
The gardens at The Manor, Hemingford
Grey, near Huntingdon, inspired Lucy
Boston's *Green Knowe* stories, so look
at the way in which the yew topiary sits
mysteriously when viewed through the
yellow flowers of the evening primrose.

Opposite page
White walls and a decked path give a clean
modernist line to the sculpted mounds of
herbs and grasses – patterns echoed in
the stained glass above the door.

Another North American medicinal herb with good flowers around
its prominent centre is the coneflower (*Echinacea*). Borage, beloved of
the ancients, is not as tall but the mass of blue star flowers delights the
eye and the spirits if you eat them. The bedstraw family includes sweet
woodruff and ladies' bedstraw, with starry flowers to brighten shady
conditions and a green blanket chorus with their whorls of leaves.

Herbs as chorus

Much has already been written about the waves of sun-loving herbs
that will create a sea of grey-greens, gold, and silver under other
plantings. There is also a good selection of shade-loving or tolerant
herbs that will create a carpet of colour. Three hardy creeping herbs in
this category are bugle, self-heal, and dead nettle, common names that
sound distinctly invasive, which indeed they can be. The white bugle
Ajuga reptans 'Alba' is the most ornamental, with dark leaves that can
provide the "black" chequer, or a foil to other spring flowers. Be
tempted by the rightly named *Prunella grandiflora* 'Loveliness', 'Pink
Loveliness', and 'White Loveliness' – the open throat of the flowers
is a clue to its medicinal use for throat infections.

If you grow the ornamental dead nettle (*Lamium maculatum*) you
will appreciate another of its common names, false salvia. It is an
astringent herb formerly prized for staunching blood like the yarrows.
Today, it is a boon plant if you are faced with inhospitable dry shade.
In a small area where high maintenance is feasible, cut it back after
flowering because you might get three crops of flower in a year. There
are silver- and golden-leaved varieties: *L. m.* 'Album' and 'Aureum'.

Groovy Grids

Twentieth-century Modernist designers reshaped the chequerboard into Mondrian, Cubist, and Abstract, blocks which in gardens take the form of paving or grass. Scent and texture can be introduced with creeping thymes, compact marjorams, flowering chives, and chamomile, or even carrots, coriander, and caraway. Grids imply linear form, squares and rectangles, and circles and crescents, and they are just the starting blocks.

Cheeky chequers

The herb gardens at the Musée de Cluny in Paris have been inspired by their medieval collections, especially the tapestries that illustrate the five senses and "my only desire". Six scenes played out on a flowery mead, the adjoining gardens follow a utilitarian monastic layout in a series of square and rectangular beds, but have literally been given a modern twist. The four symbolic waters of the Garden of Eden that divide the plantings contain a series of chromium spirals rising up to catch the light and water like the ghosts of medieval souls.

The staggered square paving and sculpted thyme so dramatically used by Californian designer Topher Delaney is illustrated on p. 51. The English designer Geoffrey Jellicoe once used a similar layout across a tiny back garden to create an illusion of far greater space.

The city of Barcelona undulates with the architecture of Antonio Gaudí, whose "trencadis" or broken colourful glazed tiles were used to decorate the buildings and their roof gardens. These mosaics of colour provide inspiration both for paving and planting; at the Parque Güell he used the massive columns that support the market place to convey rainwater into tanks to irrigate during the long hot summers. If you live in a hot dry climate, make a feature of your needs: sink the blocks to be planted, so that all surplus water will flow into them; reverse the process if your site is too damp. If the Gaudí "trencadis" effect is too garish, look to the works of fellow Catalonian Joan Miró, whose amorphous blocks of colour create illusions of space and texture.

Your wavelength

In the 17th century minds were educated in arithmetic, geometry, music, and astronomy, which inspired cosmic garden layouts of radiating rings representing the known planets. The one at Twickenham Park, near London was 90x90m (321x321ft): planet earth sat as a grass circle at its core, which the concentric circles of the moon, Mercury, and Venus were represented by the silver tones of birches; the sun and Mars warmed up to golden green shades with lime trees; then the great gods of fertility and power, Jupiter and Saturn, were captured in the blossom and fruit of fruit trees. Your first or last experience was the rosemary hedge that encompassed the design.

In Ian Hamilton Finlay's Scottish garden the word "unda", carved in pale blue and lavender letters, undulates across and up the path lined by the fern-like leaves of sweet cicely (*see p.12*). The wilderness of the Lanarkshire hills is brought into focus by carved stones that play on words; your mood and mind are altered by the juxtaposition of words carved into stone and wood with trees, flowers, herbs, grasses, and water. Also in Scotland, in the south-west, designer Charles Jencks has created a "landscape of waves" that displays the DNA double helix and no less than 15 senses. To sample just one – taste is represented by giant silver foliage lips framing a bed of alpine strawberries.

White wormwood

Sissinghurst's White Garden in Kent is laid out in a series of box-edged geometric beds, their shapes emphasized by the bright whites that abound within their framework. The garden includes some

beautiful wormwoods: *Artemesia arborescens* with delicate narrow leaves as silver as the curry plant; the diminutive silver *A. schmidana nana*; and *A. ludoviciana* with silver-grey, lance-shaped leaves. These silvery whites jostle with the pure whites of cosmos, lilies, cineraria, pear-leaved willow, *Solanum jasminoides*, nicotiana, and many more.

Thyme

Spanish gardens still echo their Moorish origins, which originated from the gardens of ancient Persia. Tours of Persia (now Iran) in the 1920s by Vita Sackville-West and Harold Nicolson inspired the Persian thyme carpet by their herb garden at Sissinghurst. Thymes lend themselves perfectly to such conceits with their range of leaf and flower colours.

The common thyme, *Thymus vulgaris*, wafts a warm, aromatic scent, is excellent for cooking, and will seed itself abundantly. It is worth making a friend of Latin names, as they often give a clue to what the plant has to offer: *sativa*, *edulis*, and *esculenta* indicate edible. The creeping wild thyme (*Thymus praecox*) flowers very early, and the hardy *Thymus serpyllum* will snake across the ground. Plant them along the edges of paths to fill every crack and crevice. The woolly thyme (*Thymus pseudolanuginosus*) is less hardy but very ornamental and tactile, forming pubescent coverlets. The broad-leaved thyme (*Thymus pulegioides*) is excellent raw in salads or as a garnish and is especially fine in summer. The stronger flavour of caraway thyme (*Thymus herba-barona*) meant that it was traditionally cooked with beef; its hardy wiry cushions are ideal for dry sunny sites. The list is endless, and, armed with secateurs or a sharp-edged spade, you can shape thyme to fit any groovy grid.

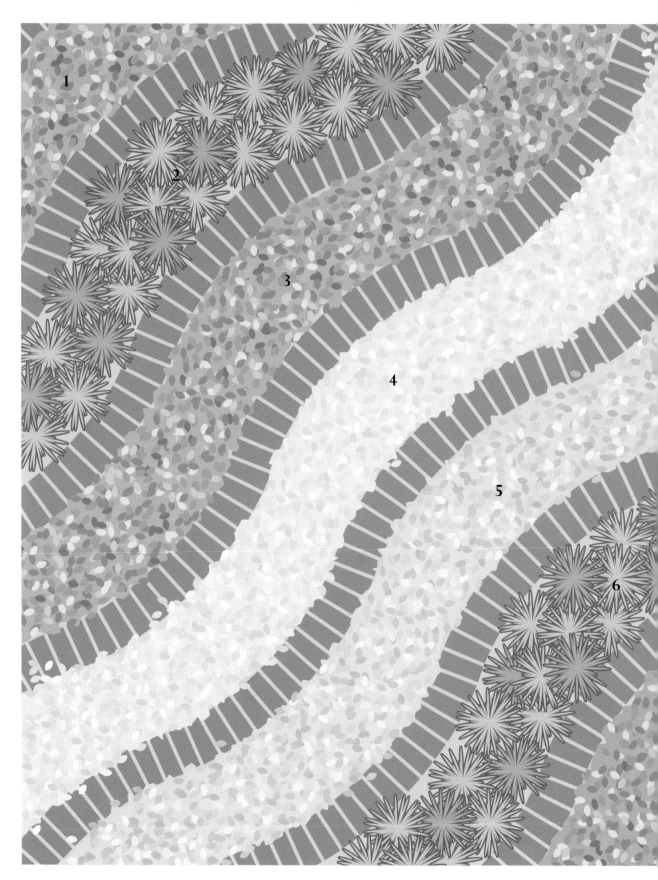

7

8

Growing in Waves

Create a grid on the ground with string or sand to provide a guide as you form your geometric curves and straight lines. It will be easier to maintain the effect if you edge each shape with bricks, setts, or metal bands.

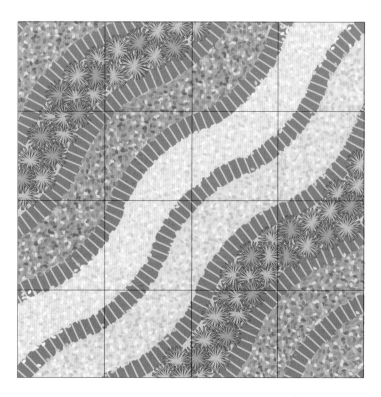

Plant list

1 Lavender-leaved sage
2 Chives
3 Purple sage
4 *Dianthus* 'Sops-in-wine'
5 Golden variegated sage
6 Ornamental *Allium moly*
7 Alpine lady's mantle
   (*Alchemilla alpina*)
8 Green sage

The effect on the left is billowing, with "waves" of cushion planting drawing the eye across the ground. Massed planting of fewer varieties creates a more dynamic style. Cut back the chives immediately after flowering, the sages early in the year, and the lady's mantle at the end of the summer.

On Top of the World

Herbs can enhance a roof, balcony, window box, or lightwell, helping to protect and improve other plantings. Next time you are in a city, look up and enjoy the surrealism of plantings against the sky. Exposure of plants to drying, damaging winds is one of the main challenges facing the rooftop gardener. Rosemary and sages, which cling to their native rock faces, readily adapt to urban breezes. Lavenders and silver-leaved thymes thrive on sunny balconies alongside cineraria, stachys, and helichrysum. The ground-hugging mints such as pennyroyal and the tiny-leaved Corsican mint will happily colonize shady bare soil with a little moisture. At a touch, the air is filled with a menthol that not only drives away flies and ants but freshens every breath you take.

Public roof

Apart from glimpsing *'murs végétals'* in Paris, and peeping down greened lightwells in Japan, I have enjoyed the ingenuity of two other roof gardens and their gardeners: that of the department store Derry and Toms in London, and the Cloisters Museum in New York. The former is served by a lift, which the gardener puts to full use bringing up compost and new plants (not to mention food for the flamingoes), and taking down weeds and debris. Herbs are dotted in and around the Moorish, Tudor, and English-styled gardens. The medieval gardens of the Cloisters Museum are truly herb gardens, with each and every plant having a use. The tapestry of herbs in the Cuxa Cloister has been overrun by periwinkle but the magnificent Bonnefont Cloister sits majestically above the Hudson River in traditional quadripartite form. The gardeners maintain the cloisters from a series of tiny rooms secreted about the perimeter – a wonder of ergonomics.

Private roof

If possible, create large, long troughs and buy good-sized containers, as these will retain moisture most effectively and absorb temperature changes gradually. Young standard shrubs and herbs adapt better than

large specimens with the added bonus of being considerably cheaper. For architectural formality as well as foliage interest, plant sweet or golden bays (*Laurus nobilis* or *L. n.* 'Aurea'), and myrtles such as the larger-leaved *Myrtus communis* or neater *M. c.* ssp. *tarentina*. Both bay and myrtle dislike frost but are reasonably wind tolerant; frost-prone plants will need to be protected with fleece or glass.

In a garden backed by a wall with a north-westerly aspect, combine myrtles with camellias in troughs filled with an ericaceous compost to provide a year-round evergreen display. If you drink tea, throw your tea leaves on the soil afterwards to benefit the camellias, which are in the same family. Keep the trough well watered in late summer, as drought will prevent good flowerbud formation. Camellias flower from late winter through to early spring in an array of colours and shapes, followed by non-edible apple-like fruits – a happy partnership with the late summer and early autumn flowering of the delicate creamy white bridal myrtle. Both myrtle and camellia respond well to either shrubby or close-clipped maintenance. The planters can be further enhanced by shade-loving bulbs or seasonal annual herbs or flowers.

For south-, east-, and west-facing areas, containers of rosemary underplanted with sage please the gardener and delight the cook. Where winters are severe, lift the containers inside until spring, then top up the compost and wait for the rosemary to finish flowering, after which you can clip and prune, preferably in early summer.

Lavenders like a bright sunny spot and good air circulation. Although more tender, the flowers of French lavender (*Lavandula stoechas*) and the butterfly or Spanish lavenders (*L. stoechas* ssp.

pedunculata) make a showy display. Hardier varieties such as the traditional spike lavenders, especially the 'Grosso' variety, should be trimmed back to buds that will grow out into a globe. This minimizes the leaves and maximizes the hedgehog effect of the flowering spikes.

The balcony scene

For balconies and window boxes you will need to examine the site's aspect carefully. It is easier to improvise shade than sun. Herbs and plants that you would use in hanging baskets are ideal for cascading out of troughs and pots down the outside of balconies and boxes. If constant watering and feeding are feasible, plant as densely as a hanging basket with bright falls of nasturtiums or scented curtains of thyme. For the cook there are red and yellow varieties of a tomato called Tumbling Toms, which fare well in hanging baskets and containers; you can add purple-leaved basils for style both on and off the plate.

The cascades will entertain passers-by but what about you looking out? If you keep a retinue of smaller containerized plants they can be moved in and out of the large trough, to take centre stage when they are at their best. Fresh potted supermarket herbs will last longer if sunk into a large pot or trough and give ornamental interest until you have picked them to extinction. Regular topping up with good compost will enable you to have catch crops of chervil, basil, and coriander.

Instead of garden furniture, why not create a "living seat" by planting a large container with a low-growing herb such as chamomile, thyme, creeping mint, or periwinkle? From this ornamental and scented vantage point you can look out on the world.

Previous pages
A living roof has been created from a planting of sedums, their succulent stems and hardy flowers ideal for the vigours of this environment.

Opposite page above
Protected by the surrounding wall and planted in deep boxes, this roof garden in New York boasts an excellent collection of thriving herbs.

Opposite page below
A boardwalk and gravel mulch set off the lavender and lovage caught in the gold light of the setting sun.

Below
The pyramid light sits among old and new rosemary bushes with an unexpected combination of fennel, mint, and chives happily colonizing the gravel.

Wafting Walls & Lurking Corners

The pleasure of enjoying the sweet savours of scented plants is, if anything, intensified in a small garden, and in rooms whose windows open out on to it. The boundaries that enclose your garden can be disguised with sun- or shade-loving climbers underplanted with aromatics, a trick I've achieved with the *Rosa rugosa* and southernwood in my driveway. With a little attention to detail you can manipulate conditions to create microclimates that provide scent for all seasons.

Going up

If you are faced with a harsh surface cover it with trellis or train your climbing plants into diaper shapes. Rosemary is the traditional wall shrub and in the right hands can be imaginatively trained. Packed into just 2ha (5 acres), La Roseraie de l'Haÿ, southeast of Paris, echoes the splendour of the Empress Josephine's gardens at Malmaison, where she had 250 rose varieties. Most spectacularly the "theatre of the rose" has roses tightly tied on and around ornate high treillage, using willow slips not plastic ties, and underplanted with yet more roses edged with clipped dwarf box. The garden's shrubby namesake rose has large, loose, crimson-purple flowers smelling of sugared almonds.

If you want to borrow the landscape or frame another part of the garden construct a catenary, which is a series of posts across which you run a rope or chain. Roses, whose soul lies in their scent, and other climbing plants can then be trained up the posts and along the rope or chain to give a swagged effect. Underplant with chives or rue, as both deter rose predators.

I have used wood and ropes and iron posts and chain but the latter can cause the plants problems in extremes of hot and cold. Roses at the Alnwick Walled Garden in Northumberland fill one corner trained along pergolas and treillage and in massed banks and beds. Anyone who feels modern roses have no fragrance should walk among its bowers. The scale is vast but the concepts and effects are readily decanted, as can be seen in the annual David Austin displays at the Philadelphia Flower Show.

Wafters

Filling the garden with wafting scents, roses, honeysuckles, jasmine, and clematis have a history and medicinal qualities that must class them as herbs. At the top of our drive we have planted the winter honeysuckle (*Lonicera fragrantissima*) and *Viburnum* x *bodnantense* 'Dawn', whose wafting scents on cold nights provide a warm welcome. The Ruined Arch at the Royal Botanic Gardens, Kew, is swathed in the perfectly named climbing shrub wintersweet (*Chimonanthus praecox*), not to be mistaken for the sub-shrub wintergreen (*Gaultheria procumbens*), whose summer pinky-white flowers are followed by aromatic red berries that last throughout the winter. The latter was used by Native Americans for aches and pains — you could try adding a few of the glossy elliptic leaves to your tea.

The drug mezereon was extracted from *Daphne mezereum* but is no longer considered safe. However, the scented red and, more rarely, white flowers of the so-called February daphne are perfectly safe and sweetly scented in winter. The March air at the Atlanta Botanical Gardens, Georgia, is assailed by the sweet scent of the deep pink flowers of the Himalayan daphne (*D. bholua*). For a subtler spring fragrance you could also grow *D. genkwa*, whose use in Chinese medicine dates back to 1,500 BC. All will grow in borders, providing a green backdrop, when other shrubs and herbaceous perennials start to make a show.

Previous pages
Looking as good as they smell the
thorny rugosa rose underplanted with
southernwood wafts delicious scent
up across our driveway in Suffolk.

Opposite page above
A simple seat tempts you to sit down and
breathe in the aroma of sage and lavender
in Brita von Schoenaich's design.

Opposite page below
Joanna Reed was a consummate gardener,
cook, and embroiderer, as is aptly
illustrated by her herb parterre at
Longview Farm, Pennsylvania.

Above
The fresh scent of spring can be enjoyed
as the flowers of lily of the valley open
among bluebells and navelwort
(*Omphalodes cappadocica* 'Cherry Ingram')
in Carol Klein's garden in Devon.

Lurkers

Try to create corners and pockets that catch the sun, especially in winter, then plant them up with aromatic creeping and crevice herbs such as thyme, mint, calamint, and compact marjoram. Chamomile seats do not have to be fashioned out of timber, brickwork, or stone, just plant up cushioned seats in rockeries or between tree roots. The apple scent is gently fragrant until you step or sit on it, when it attaches itself to you, leaving you to waft pleasantly on. We have gravel and rocks loosely arranged around the base of our 70-year-old Williams pear tree, and for several years I had two chamomile seats for my nephews in the root hollows. Now I have pockets of lavender-leaved sage, the black-leaved *Ophiopogon*, marjoram, bulbs, and a *Clematis orientalis* 'Bill MacKenzie' climbing into the tree canopy.

Lily of the valley is both a lurking and wafting scent during the warmer days of late spring. I have winter savory for winter pickings and late summer flowers and the sweetly scented double 'Mrs Sinkins'

pinks growing around it. Once you have planted sweet violet it will
happily colonize and seed itself; the variety 'Princess of Wales' has
large, deep purple flowers and the sweetest fragrance. The white-
flowering form now creates spring-scented pools under our
hornbeam arbour. The flowers are also delicious in salads.

Courtyards and cloisters

Travelling through Japan by train gives you the chance to glimpse how
the smallest corners are used to nurture plants. Visits to traditional
temples and shrines sculpt your vision into simple shapes but complex
thoughts, each plant playing a balanced part with stones, wood, and
raked surfaces. Staying in a ryokan, a traditional Japanese inn, you
may well have your own tiny private courtyard to look out on.

During the winter the Cloisters Museum in New York puts up
sealed glass screens around the Bonnefont and other cloisters, the
scene within enlivened by a range of containerized scented shrubs,
herbs, and bulbs. Large quantities of bay and myrtle are brought in to
create garlands to decorate the museum's interior.

The courtyards at Brief, in Sri Lanka, flank the house on all sides,
the tropical climate allowing only decorative ironwork to separate
inner from garden rooms. A nursery holds containerized plants that
can be brought out when they are at their best. This is a garden where
tropical exuberance meets European formality infused with Buddhist
simplicity. Exotic fruits range alongside jasmines and frangipanes.

Arbours

In the herb garden at the Geffrye Museum in London, peace and a room within a room is provided by the traditional arbours over which jasmine and honeysuckle have been trained. Jasmine can be styled to suit every season and situation, from the yellow, winter-flowering form to the exotically scented tender Sambac variety. Jasmine has always been associated with arbours, shaded retreats, and covered walks; it also makes an excellent wall shrub if clipped hard after flowering.

Gather the flowers to express your feelings: white for amiability and yellow for grace and elegance. More exotically and erotically, in Chinese, Batavian, and Hindu cultures the flowerbuds were rolled into well-oiled hair, so that the scents were slowly and increasingly exuded during the day and night with aphrodisiac effects.

Favourites

Other choice plants to add to the list include: the wafting fragrances of the autumn-flowering tree *Clerodendron* and evening primrose, and the lurking scents of *Eucalyptus gunnii*, golden marjoram, *Hyssopus officinalis*, sweet bay, *Lavandula dentata*, lemon balm, lemon verbena, and catmint.

Opposite page
The pinks and whites of the gloriously fragrant and textured rambling roses are echoed by the long scented trumpets of the honeysuckle.

Below
Water lilies can be grown to cover lakes or simply to adorn a small water feature. Many have a light fragrance.

The Salad Basket

Thirty years ago vegetable guru Joy Larkcom set out to sample the salad delights of Europe and, among many discoveries, returned with seeds of the Lollo Rosso lettuce. Ten years ago a basket-maker wove a large wicker fence around a summer potager for Larkcom's former Suffolk garden. The curvaceous boundary protected the summer crops and yet allowed a good circulation of air and exposure to all available sunshine. Low wattle fences have recently enjoyed a revival – although only relatively short-lived they allow the gardener to build up the soil without it spilling over into the surrounding gravel or grass. A huge basket complete with handle has been created on a corner site at Waddesdon Manor in Buckinghamshire. It has been planted up with herbs and vegetables including squash. If you choose a final crop of pumpkins or pattypans, use the rich blank soil for a catch crop of lettuce, salad rocket, chervil, coriander, and dill. Recent research has shown that there is more goodness from eating cooked spinach and cabbage – purely because you will eat larger quantities – but freshly harvested salad herbs offer supercharged vitamin and mineral boosts to the body.

Salading and dressing

I divide herbs into salading herbs, which are good coarsely chopped or torn as a visual, textual, tastily recognizable part of a salad, and dressing herbs which are finely chopped to impart flavour to oils, vinegar, vinaigrette, mayonnaise, and a host of other salad dressings. Make up small quantities frequently as they do not keep well. They are also invaluable in the preparation of low-salt foods – minimizing or replacing any need for salt.

The problem with designing a salad basket is that, if it is fulfilling its purpose, you will be creating gaps as you constantly harvest the crops. So keep the soil fertile and regularly scatter sow quick-fix herbs such as chervil, dill, which coriander that will germinate rapidly and are best eaten young. Plain-leaved parsley, salad rocket, and 'Lettuce

Previous pages
Note the shell detail and mulch of stones that gives a salty sensation to the salad edging of lettuces.

Right
In Yokohama, Japan, Seiko Hirota created this look in just one year. The blue edging boards and wattle fencing hold in abundance with good taste.

Below
At Hampton Court, in Herefordshire, the large-leaved 'Indian Giant' parsley and lettuces are brightened by the bright orange Californian poppies.

Leaf' lettuces are good for edging because you pick their leaves rather than the whole head; look out for the 'Lollo Mixed', which has green and red leaves, or the oak-leaved 'Red Salad Bowl', and 'Cocarde'.

Mint has plenty of ornamental uses but in a salad bed it is better grown in its own basket! The young tips of mint are especially good in cucumber salads in traditional combinations such as raita (cucumber, yogurt, and mint). Find a place for garlic – if you plant plenty on the shortest day of the year you can start harvesting green garlic as soon as it starts shooting. Leave them until summer when they should be mature enough to form large bulbs.

Leafy herbs

In a flower garden herbs can seem subtly coloured, but put them among salad vegetables, and they seem positively kaleidoscopic. You may not choose to eat a plate of dandelion or rocket leaves but their flavour alongside other leaves refreshes and enhances the whole salad. The consumption of dill, sorrel, and dandelions is claimed to renew vigour, so you can throw out the Viagra. Many herbs are at their tender best during the traditional "hungry gap" in spring; this includes sweet cicely, which you will only want to eat for their young leaves then leave them to become ornamental. The round crenated leaves of the salad burnet are delightful scattered in a green salad but they must be young and fresh as the older leaves are dry and papery. On the other hand, the celery-flavoured and leafed lovage is worth keeping cut back throughout the summer to maintain young leaves.

Early in the spring bronze fennel is such a dark purple that it looks like a black feathery fern and it has a mouth-tingling aniseed flavour. You can try to keep this from flowering in order to prolong the leaf harvest but you will lose the advantages of its height. The sweet fennel has clear green fresh leaves but let it grow up and form delicious yellow flowerheads and seeds; both can be used to take the compositional effect upwards and out of the salad basket.

If your garden enjoys warmth and plenty of summer sunshine try different varieties of basil such as the purple-veined 'Anise' and 'Cinnamon', and the deep purple 'Dark Opals'. Beware of shredding 'Green Ruffles' or they will look like caterpillars in your green salad. All of these are attractive enough to be used as summer bedding plants that can be harvested as and when you want them. If you still have plenty as the frosts approach, cut them to the ground and freeze the whole stems.

The delicate greens of coriander are visually attractive. Choose a good, leaf-forming variety such as 'Cilantro' and keep picking to stop it going to flower as well as sowing successively. If it does go to flower, just leave the pale pink umbels to create a gauzy haze among the other salads. A more feathery dark green is provided by dill: 'Dukat' is the best leaf form, whereas 'Mammoth', as the name suggests, will grow very tall with saucer-sized umbels and masses of seed.

Nasturtiums provide colour and will grow in the driest conditions; the flowers and leaves are very peppery but delicious in a green salad. The white marbled leaves of the 'Alaska' series are less peppery, and the dark, almost purple, leaves and red flowers of 'Empress of India' are decidely ornamental. The green and golden purslanes deserve to be grown and eaten much more – their slightly succulent leaves are refreshing and give texture to a green salad.

The acid lemon taste of sorrel can be enjoyed throughout late spring and summer – constant picking will stop the large-leafed French varieties from going to seed. The tidier buckler-leafed sorrels *Rumex scutatus*, and *R.s.* 'Silver Shield' have smaller leaves that can be picked and scattered into a green salad. They prefer shade and will tolerate dry conditions.

Last, but not least, marjorams and thymes will never let you down. From the more tender aromatic Greek oregano to gold and compact forms of both, however much you pick them they will still look, smell, and taste good and should be the backbone of any culinary design. Modern research has shown, the more you eat thyme, the longer the ageing process will take.

Flowery feasts

The leaves of salad rocket have a nutty, radish-like taste but the pale lemon crucifer flowers and flowerbuds are better by far – nutty, succulent, and slightly fragrant. The starry flowers of borage are equally good in green or fruit salads but always extract the flower from its backing, as this has a dry leafy texture. Stagger your cull of chives so that you cut from one or two clumps at a time – that way you should have leaves and possibly flowers from late spring onwards. Chives are easy to divide: lift in spring and separate into as many units as you want clumps. The flowerheads, common, pink, white, or Chinese, should be divided into individual florets before eating. The orange petals of the French marigold (*Calendula officinalis*) and the bright red, yellow, and orange flowers of nasturtiums bring fiery colour to the garden and the plate. Sweet violets, blue and white, have a crisp texture and taste like violet creams, so scatter them over a salad.

Dressing herbs

Finely chopped to give a cordon vert touch to any dish these herbs can be grown alongside complementary vegetables, such as summer savory and beans, or dotted in with other plantings, which are more conveniently positioned near an outer door. Top of the list must be French, never Russian, tarragon, which transforms any salad, fish, chicken, or egg dish. Any of the fine-leafed basils such as the bush, fine, and lemon varieties can be grown in terracotta pots. Always include the stems of basil and parsley, as they will give extra flavour.

Already mentioned, and as useful whole as chopped, are chervil, all varieties of chives, dill, fennel, and marjoram. They can also be harvested to flavour oil and vinegar as can elder and lavender flowers, Remove all herbs after steeping and decorate with dried herbs.

The leaves of many baby vegetables are excellent in salads so if you grow greens try nibbling the young leaves of brassicas and chard. Apart from the pleasure of watching your edible feast growing, the harvest for your plate is just as exciting for one person as a dozen.

Herb and leafy vegetable seeds can be sown in small baskets to create microsalads, which are harvested just as the first and second true leaves appear. When a seed germinates, it first anchors its root, then puts out two small seedling leaves; when sufficiently established, the first true leaves, that is those that are typical, are formed. This is an upmarket version of mustard and cress on a flannel or blotting paper and can be done on a windowsill. The spun-sugar effect of green and purple stems and the zesty taste provides a refreshing appetiser.

Opposite page
The Gardener's Labyrinth at Yalding Organic Gardens in Kent has a radiating maze of edible beds – nasturtium, lettuce, orache, artichokes, and beneficial insect attractants such as the lavender flowered fiddleneck.

Below
A flour pot sprouts mizuna greens in photographer Marianne Majerus' garden in London.

Cordials & Aphrodisiacs

The island of Ischia lies just over the bay from Naples in Italy, and
spiritually it is totally removed from the mayhem of Neapolitan dust
and traffic. From 1956 Sir William Walton composed here and his
wife, Susana Walton, with the help of Russell Page, carved a garden of
tropical splendour out of its rugged rocks. The hill carried the name of
Le Mortelle, which in Neapolitan dialect becomes *mortella*, or myrtle,
with visions of Aphrodite seeking refuge in a divine myrtle grove after
emerging from the foam. Lady Walton harvests the leaves to flavour
food and makes a liqueur from the berries, which among other uses
flavours water ices. The now-famous gardens of La Mortella are, like
their doyenne, *con brio,* but the myrtle was there first, which, in Lady
Walton's words, "sprouts with great abandon from the crevices
between the boulders on the hill and delights everybody."

Purple hearts

Traditionally, a cordial was taken to strengthen the heart. In the 1980s
plans were drawn up at one of the colleges of Glasgow University for
a medicinal garden, whose beds were to be shaped like the different
internal organs and planted up with their associated curative herbs.
The heart has always been a popular motif. At Squerryes Court in
Kent the heart outline is formed in dwarf box and only filled with
massed purple sage – inspired not by hallucinogenic purple hearts
but an early 18th-century design.

   The symbolism of the heart was taken a step further by Joachim
Carvallo at Villandry in the Loire Valley, in France. There are four
squares set around a fountain (the source of eternal life and love), and
each has a different box-hedged heart motif to warn you of the perils
of love and lust. The first square for tender love has four hearts filled
with pink flowers licked by tiny flames and white-flowered lips
whispering sweet nothings. The pace hots up in the second square,
with pink-, white-, and yellow-flowered heart shapes dancing a
tarantella within their design of passionate love. The third sounds

the path to ruin: here, there no hearts, just the horns of lust, fans behind which gossips hide, and a torn-up telltale love letter, all box hedged and filled with yellow and white flowers. The fourth and final sombre square has red flowers, a broken heart at its core, with "blood-soaked" daggers and swords that symbolize the inevitable outcome of tragic love.

You might want to take the symbolism a step further and edge a heart with low "stepover" apple trees or a taller outer ring; choose varieties with decorative blossom and good fruit such as the nutty flavoured russets 'Ashmead's Kernel' or 'Rosemary Russet'.

Cordials and infusions

Elderflowers and mint both make delicious cordials: the elder could be the centrepiece of a large heart, especially if you select a golden or dark, purple-leafed variety. A cordial from elderberries is packed with vitamin C and – if mixed with hot water – makes a wonderful winter warmer. Mints are perfect for massed planting: a heart filled with the white variegated applemint and edged with the creamy-flowered cotton lavender 'Lemon Queen' would be light and bright from late spring until winter. Mixing the white, gold, and purple-streaked mints sounds effective but one will rapidly dominate – their leaf textures are all different, so if you are prepared for biennial lifting and splitting it is worth a try. Pour boiling syrup over chopped mint leaves and leave to steep to make a cordial or sorbet base. Mint with borage is essential for any Pimms mixture; in drinks, use the borage leaves as well as the flowers, which impart a light cucumber flavour. Borage is reputed to stimulate the adrenalin, renew vigour, and cheer you up, so try grazing the flowers each time you pass. Borage and strawberries, both the alpine and dessert varieties, grow well together. In the Evening Gardens section (*see pp.64-71*) I recommend the ornamental variegated strawberry, *Fragaria* x *ananassa variegata* – for good flavour try 'Pegasus' or 'Rhapsody'. We have white-berried alpine strawberries, which are so sweet they taste like white chocolate.

The massed star-like flowers of sweet woodruff thrive in dappled shade, and the plant is at its best in late spring and early summer. In Germany the flowering stems of woodruff are mixed with strawberries and white wine. With or without the strawberries, sweet woodruff infuses an aromatic fragrance and acts as a physical tonic.

Aphrodisiacs

When potatoes were first introduced into Britain, one of the by-lines was that they had aphrodisiac qualities; from this we can deduce that an important element of any plant deemed an "aphrodisiac" is probably how rare it is, how it is served, and with whom you take it. You could say the same for the aphrodisiac recipe that calls for lettuce leaves and the powdered genitalia of a timid bull. Warm evenings and the sweet scent of jasmine would be a good finale but good health and happiness make the best starter.

Drinking jasmine tea has a sedative effect, as does the scent of jasmine oil when used in aromatherapy. According to the 17th-century herbalist and astrologist, Nicolas Culpeper, "Jessamine is a warm cordial plant, governed by Jupiter in the sign of Cancer...It disperses crude humours...The oil is good also for hard and contracted limbs, it opens, warms, and softens the nerves and tendons."

Previous pages
A window on the world of the sage-, santolina-, and lavender-filled hearts and squares at Squerryes Court in Kent.

Above
The fragrant blossoms of sweet woodruff planted under golden hop look their best here and are ready for steeping in drinks.

Opposite page
Lobelia 'Bees', a colourful reminder of the medicinal risks our ancestors took – light the touch paper and stand back!

Roses are red…yellow, and white

The rose, renewal, and regeneration are symbolically associated with Aphrodite or Venus as she stepped from the foam. The warm moist winds of the Zephyr brought spring to the Classical world, the green blade rising with leaves full of green (*khloros*), love (*philos*), or, more scientifically, chlorophyll. In his *Birth of Venus*, Botticelli shows Flora, who was the wood nymph Chloris before being transformed by Zephyr, now depicted blowing moist air onto Venus, and trying to cover Venus with a floral cloak while the heavens rain roses. As the days lengthen and warm, Venus, like the rosebud, starts to unfold her beauty and reveal the flowering of her heart.

The apothecary's rose was prized for its medicinal virtues, as were the later damask and alba roses. Roses and herbs are a natural combination. All rose petals can be eaten but the different textures may affect your choice. Many recipes call for the removal of the yellow heels on petals, although personally I have never found them too strong. My favourites are the rich fragrant petals of 'Penelope' or 'Zéphirine Drouhin' scattered over a Sephardic chocolate cake.

Fragrance is a must followed by continuous or repeat-flowering and disease resistant roses. The new cupped pink flowers of 'Alnwick Castle' have an old rose scent with a hint of raspberry. The heavenly, scented burgundy-coloured rose 'Souvenir du Docteur Jamain' needs a canopy of dappled shade to thrive and repeat flower in the autumn; underplant with alliums, sweet cicely, or clary sages.

Roses are the flowers of poetry and beauty, with which you can express 34 different sentiments of love, distain, or even rejection. A rosebud is an expression of "young and innocent love" and stems with leaves mean that "the recipient may still hope on". Growing and then presenting the fruity scented red 'Benjamin Britten' will say "I love you" but the more formal-shaped, deeper purplish red 'Prospero' means "bashful shame". A white rose such as the ancient *Rosa alba*, known as 'Maiden's Blush' in English and 'Nymph's Thighs' in French, simply means "silence, I am worthy of you" but if withered "transient impressions". Yellow roses may be good for Texans but the wonderfully fragrant 'Dutch Gold' or climbing 'The Garland' symbolize "jealousy" or "a decrease of love". One of my fragrant favourites is the climber 'Zéphirine Drouhin', whose thornless stems and deep pink flowers offer "early attachment". The eglantine growing in our hedge is a "symbol of true love because it survives happiness and adversity".

These messages can be expanded by including the other plant sacred to Venus, the myrtle, symbol of pure love and a happy marriage; plus rosemary for remembrance and fidelity in love; and pansies for thoughts. Carnations can send out mixed messages: the traditional deep red means "alas for my poor heart", whereas a striped flower signals "refusal" and a yellow one "disdain". Two herbs that can be woven into any planting scheme are ivy and periwinkle: the former is a sign of friendship, fidelity, and marriage, while the latter represents happy recollections. To keep the symbols of love alive overwinter plant daphnes, which mean the "desire to please", with snowdrops – a "gentle 'no thank you' but an emblem of consolation and hope in life" – followed by blue hyacinths as a symbol of fidelity. Columbines signal unchastness, and the yellow umbels of fennel deceit but the last straw in every sense must be to send a straw to someone to signal "suffer me to be your slave".

Previous pages
The roots of the coneflower (*Echinacea*) have become of increasing medicinal importance for boosting the immune system. They also make attractive additions to any garden.

Above
A cordial arrangement in every sense: harvest the borage flowers and leaves and then try drinking a potion from "the poor man's medicine chest" – cabbage.

Opposite page
The silver bracts of the sea holly will catch the moonlight when you are searching out borage leaves and flowers for an evening drink.

Jungle Herbs

You do not need tropical heat and humidity to grow dramatic large herbs; their leaf size will be dictated by how much moisture there is in the soil and not necessarily their height. The art is to take on potential thugs and perfect their performance so that no soil shows. If you live in a seasonal climate, these herbs will reach their zenith in late spring and summer, and many will disappear as winter approaches.

The statuesque

The tallest herbs will tower above their surrounding plantings giving Gaudíesque architectural spires. Two Japanese esculent herbs are viewed as thugs in the West: the *gobo* or burdock, and *fuki* or butterbur. The burdock (*Arctium lappa*) is a robust biennial with stout, edible tap roots, which means once it has established it is unmoveable until it dies; the seedlings are easily recognizable. Burdock has large dock-like leaves, and the purple bristly flowers are followed by hooked fruits or "burs", which attach themselves to absolutely everything. The butterbur or sweet coltsfoot (*Petasites japonicus* and *P. j.* var. *giganteus*) rising to 1–2m (1–6½ft) should be left to make stately colonies in bog gardens. The flower buds, *kokinato*, are considered Japanese delicacies. The pale pink flowering winter heliotrope (*P. fragrans*), which grows to about 30cm (12in), flourishes in warm dry conditions, giving out a vanilla scent in winter; in colder areas it can be raised in a container.

In 2002 there was a spate of ricin poisonings in England, ricin being the active ingredient in the seed coat of the ornamental castor-oil plant (*Ricinus communis*). The triffid shape, large palmate leaves, and curiously clustered flowerheads all coated in a vivid red down make the castor-oil plant a key feature in any exotic bedding scheme. Along with bananas, grasses, and *Verbena bonariensis* they create a tropical look, as can be seen in Christopher Lloyd's garden at Great Dixter in Sussex or on the Isle of Wight at the Ventnor Botanical Gardens.

Mulleins (*Verbascum* spp.) will march across any design happily self-seeding, leaving instantly recognizable downy leaves. *V. olympicum* may

take two years to fully develop but the finished plant has a woolly rosette 1m (3ft) across with majestic stems reaching 1.8m (6ft) and more. Yellow spires framed in white tapers are standard fare but you can also get pinks, purples, and whites. Teasels (*Dipsacus* spp.) will grow in heavy clay, their bristly stems and cone flowerheads rising in rural majesty. You can either pick the flowerheads for displays or leave them to attract gold finches and, of course, seed themselves everywhere.

Warfarin, used both to kill rats and thin human blood, was discovered in the fungal growth on damp stems of melilot dried in hay for fodder. Melilot will seed itself vigorously but being in the pea family it helps fix nitrogen in the soil and has a pleasant wild appearance with masses of tiny yellow lathyrus flowers.

Distant spires

Native North American medicinal herbs such as Jo-pye weed, goldenrod, great lobelia, and bugbane are equally suited to wild or border conditions. Jo-pye weed (*Eupatorium maculatum* and

E. purpureum) reaching 2–3m (6½–10ft) fill the back of a border with densely flowering panicles, as well as providing a useful nectar source for bees and butterflies – hence its other name of queen of the meadow. When the series of walled gardens or *chartreuses* at the Château Canon in Normandy were first restored in the 1990s, massed plantings of goldenrod (*Solidago* spp.) were used to cover the bare earth and give golden vistas. The yellow massed daisy flowers attract many beneficial insects, including lacewings and ladybirds, which are invaluable in the war against aphid depredation.

The traditional medicinal use for great lobelia persists in its Latin name (*Lobelia siphilitica*); today, let it run along the back of a border to provide late-summer blues. It is very tolerant of dry conditions and has white and purple flowering forms. Requiring richer, moister conditions is bugbane (*Cimicifuga racemosa*), with long spires of white flowers.

European natives, including the herb that supposedly sprang from Helen of Troy's tears, elecampane (*Inula helenium*), meadowsweet (*Filipendula ulmaria*), and valerian (*Valeriana officinalis*) also need moist conditions. The downy broad leaves of elecampane are followed by shaggy yellow flowers; its roots were formerly used to make a cordial.

Meadowsweet naturalizes along ditches, the creamy-white plumes filling the summer air with a heady orange flower scent. The common or true valerian should not be mistaken for the drought-tolerant red valerian (*Centranthus* spp.). Valerian is found worldwide except in Australia and provides a tall swaying mass of pinky-white flower clusters reaching 1.5m (5ft) in summer. The root is still used medicinally and is supposed to deter rodents and cats.

Previous pages
The height and density of the pink flowerheads of Jo-pye weed are balanced in the corners of Brita von Schoenaich's design in Oxfordshire.

Above
The moat at Bedfield Hall, Suffolk, is edged with a profusion of the day lilies 'Golden Chimes' and 'Amersham', poppies, astilbes, and, in the driest part, sea hollies.

Right
The fern foliage of bronze fennel acts like a lacy screen in front of this Normandy window – now would be the time to eat the flowers.

Above
At Helmingham Hall in Suffolk, love-in-a-mist has self-sown vigorously, throwing its finely woven web of leaves around the other plants.

Right
In the woodland garden at Vann, in Surrey, Ramsons garlic and comfrey create a dense spring green-and-white carpet.

Green leaves

Just a few of each of the following plants will instantly hide a shed or wood pile for most of the spring and summer. Plant angelica, sweet cicely, lovage, and sweet woodruff as a dramatic foliage group – all benefit from a moisture-retentive soil. In spring they are all delicious to eat or drink before they fill out with voluptuous green abundance.

The much-despised ground elder has an attractive variegated form, which is just as hard to eradicate but you can eat it until it flowers, and it covers bare earth at speed. Ideal for an awkward corner, most winter bulbs, including crocus, snowdrops, and even narcissus, will break through the network of root runners to give colour early in the year.

Eating your weeds is one way of controlling many jungle herbs, especially lemon balm, which has recently been shown to cheer you up and sharpen your wits. Do not allow it to flower, just keep it as a trimmed mound; the golden forms are attractive.

Mints

The nymph, Menthe, attracted the attentions of Pluto, the god of the Underworld, much to the annoyance of his wife Persephone. Menthe found herself taken to the entrance of the Underworld and metamorphosed into a mint plant. To this day it thrives in damp shady places. As the summer season progresses mints send up their pinky-mauve flowerheads from a range of different leaf shapes and shades. The purple and red-veined medicinal mints, peppermint and red raripila, are smooth and digestive. The green 'Crispa' mint provides a crinkled textural contrast with other plantings, as does the white variegated applemint. Bowles mint can be variable – for maximum effect the leaves should be thickly pubescent, so that they gleam by moonlight and give a whitish-green contrast during the day.

The closely related bergamot, if planted in good, moisture-retentive soil, will reward you with shaggy red flowers; these and its pink and white hybrids will provide drifts of scented colour.

There are several groundcover mints – the pennyroyals and Corsican mints. The common pennyroyal (*Mentha pulegium*) will rampage in damp spots but is an excellent fly and ant repellent. Tidier and more ornamental is the 'Cunningham Mint' form and the more pungent native Australian, *Mentha satureioides*. The tiny Corsican mint (*Mentha requienii*) has been put to excellent use between the paviors at the Nunobiki terrace gardens above Kobe in Japan (*see p.90*).

Spring fillers

The greater and lesser celandines are from two different families but both are invaluable for leaf and flower interest. The greater celandine (*Chelidonium majus*) has downy, pale green oak-like leaves, which in my garden gently disguise the bare stems of the hybrid musk roses. It has a bright orange sap that can be used on warts and corns. The flowers are insignificant, and I usually weed out most of the plants once the roses have plenty of leaves. In her gardens in Essex, Beth Chatto lets the bright yellow lesser celandine (*Ranunculus ficaria*) carpet her spring beds and then die back to nothing. Finally, if you have some shady damp soil leave Ramsons garlic to colonize; you will be rewarded with the fresh smells of garlic and myriad white flowers in late spring. Too strong in flavour to eat, it can be steeped in wine as a medicinal tonic.

Fast Food

Many years ago I designed a herb garden for a client whose primary interest was cooking. He wanted the garden arranged into meat, chicken, fish, sauce, and salad herb beds that would also look good. The area was 4.5x3m (15x10ft), east and south facing, and surrounded with a low wall. I designed central diamonds for meat, chicken, and fish, with side beds for the sauce and dressing herbs.

Another client asked for the herbs to be designed into the shape of the food for which they could be used. Inspired by one of the themes at the Michigan 4H Children's Garden in the United States, I designed a pizza garden, shaped in a circle, growing the ingredients for a classic pizza. I also devised a club sandwich and salad bowl. At La Chattonière in the Loire Valley the kitchen garden, or garden of abundance, is in the shape of a leaf bountifully filled with herbs and salad vegetables.

Take-away convenience

The woody herbs found in a bouquet garni are best for long, slow cooking; *herbes provençales*, when slowly cooked, will aromatically and fragrantly evoke a taste of the Mediterranean and, if chopped very finely, can be briefly cooked; while *fines herbes* can be used raw or cooked. All these kitchen herbs will fare well in large containers – either terracotta pots or half barrels or a good-sized window box – but they all need good light conditions. If the area around your kitchen door is unpropitious, double up the containers and rotate them so that they can recuperate in a sunny spot.

If herbs are to serve as fast food they need to be near to hand and easy to gather. A long diaper or ladder-shaped bed would be ideal along a path or terrace, with each pocket reserved for a different herb. In Gloucestershire, Rosemary Verey created a delightful diaper bed with open sides, so that the cushion herbs fell over the path that led from her kitchen. The outline of the diapers or ladder could be created with any of the culinary herbs discussed in the section on herb boundaries (*see pp. 72–7*), or simply with dwarf box.

Previous pages
The flowers of chamomile can be infused
into tea that will calm your whole system
quickly, and enable you to digest and sleep.

Above
The Rainbow Garden at the Michigan 4H
Children's Garden has a kaleidoscopic
racial arrangement of native American
and introduced flowers and food crops.

Opposite page
The simplest ideas are often the best as in
the Garden of Abundance at La Chattonière
in the Loire Valley. The garden has been
designed in the shape of a leaf, the veins
formed by the path.

The bouquet garni

The key herbs for meat are bay, thyme, marjoram, and parsley; for
chicken: bay, lemon thyme, marjoram, parsley, and French tarragon;
for fish: bay, lemon thyme or lemon balm, and fennel; for white sauces
just bay but for tomato-or stock-based sauces bay use marjoram and
basil as well. Gather a bunch of herbs and tie them with undyed string
or white cotton or wrap in a leek leaf; place with the ingredients to be
cooked but remove the bouquet garni before serving.

The centrepiece has to be a bay bush – ideally the sweet bay needs
morning shade in case of frost and can be hard clipped. The golden bay
has a more delicate flavour, and can also be hard clipped, and, although
its leaves will catch the frost, it seems hardier than the green bay so it
can be grown in a more open position. You could arrange the other
herbs in circles or grids around it, according to how much you need: try
an outer edging of lemon and common thyme; then, golden marjoram
and annually enriched soil for parsley. Fennel would be an alternative or
joint centrepiece, and lemon balm must be kept under control by
frequent picking. French tarragon needs winter protection and a well-
drained site; plant it in late spring, when the danger of frost is passed.
Apart from these last three, the rest should be available year-round.

Herbes provençales

What gives Mediterranean food its warm fragrant flavour? All the
traditional sun-loving herbs: bay, thyme, rosemary, oregano, lavender,
and hyssop plus basil and parsley. If you have a dry rocky part of the
garden colonize it with these hardy spiky herbs or blocks of them in

paving or terracing. At Hestercombe Gardens in Somerset the lavenders have clung to the south-facing wall for decades, and even in the chill heights of Hardstoft Herbs in Derbyshire thyme manages to cascade down the west-facing raised bed.

Design the planting in raised beds along a south-facing wall or brick path, perhaps near a barbecue so that you can harvest the rosemary branches to become kebab skewers. Trim back the woody, leafless branches of thyme, hyssop, and lavender to burn on the barbeque. Use the leaves in marinades or scatter them over whatever is being barbecued.

Fines herbes

This classic combination is made up of chives, French tarragon, parsley, and chervil. These herbs are ideal for growing in a large pot or their own wicker-edged bed. Chives just need regular cutting to maintain fine spikes. French tarragon is perennial with an aniseed flavour and clear soft leaves. Parsley can be left for a year or two, and, once established, chervil will self-seed – at the beginning it is worth

staggering the sowing so that you have regular supplies. Scatter *fines herbes* into a sandwich or fold into an omelette but never cook for too long – the shorter the better – as you will capture the fresh aromatics perfectly. All four herbs also freeze very well.

Pizza garden

As mentioned on p.125, this is annually created at the Michigan 4H Children's Garden within a wheel minus one slice. The melting cheese is represented by the French marigold (*Tagetes patula*), which falls over and softens the stone (bread) edging. For the tomatoes Michigan recommend Roma VF, large tomatoes such as beefsteak, or 'Tumbling Tom Yellow'. You must include onions on the pizza, and here Michigan 4H keep up the colour interest by using sets of red, white, or yellow varieties. Capsicums are included, usually the sweet bell peppers, although you could experiment with jalapenos and habaneros for an eye-watering experience. Then there is a good sprinkling of basil, using attractive varieties such as 'Dark Opal', 'Purple Ruffles', 'Green Ruffles', 'Anise', and the lemon, purple or green Japanese basil (*Perilla* spp.). Try true Greek oregano (*Origanum onites*) or other attractive varieties, including the compact (*O. vulgare compactum*), American variegated marjoram 'Well-Sweep', and golden marjoram. Moss-curled parsley will look more attractive than plain-leaved. No combination like this would be complete without bush or cushion-forming thyme but avoid creeping varieties. Look out for the ornamental and delicious 'Archer's Gold', 'Silver Posie', and the golden variegated and broad-leaved thyme.

Coriander

In 1998 I joined the Herb Society of America to judge the herbs in the Pennsylvanian Horticultural Society's autumn Harvest Show, and was introduced to three totally different plants, all labelled coriander. What I instantly recognized as coriander (*Coriandrum sativum*) was lush and green. The next herb had a small cone-like flower that looked like a diminutive sea holly. It proved to be *Eryngium foetidum*, known as culantro, fitweed, or false coriander. It is found seasonally in the West Indies, Central America, and Florida, and in fact was being exhibited by someone from the Caribbean who had grown it in a greenhouse. The taste is similar to that of the common coriander or cilantro but is much stronger. It is much used in Latin American food and is being increasingly used in South-East Asian cooked dishes. The third coriander was a knotweed or bistort (*Polygonum odoratum*) or Vietnamese coriander *rau ram*, which I have also eaten in Japan under the name *baday*. It has a lemony coriander flavour, and is added to meat and chicken dishes, duck eggs, and a cabbage mixture called *du'a cân*.

Opposite page
The deep purple Japanese basil is routinely served with raw fish. Modern research has shown that it is a natural antidote to food poisoning from eating raw fish.

Below
Galvanized containers make a novel and eye-catching way of growing herbs by the kitchen door. However, you must ensure that they have drainage holes.

Shaping Up

In a hard landscape of buildings and paving, specimen trees and shrubs help to soften the edges. In a country cottage garden packed with jostling flowers, the colourful haze can be brought into focus by clipped topiary. In the Garden District of New Orleans there is a wealth of planters flanking smartly painted front doors, typically a balanced pair of clipped evergreens such as bay, myrtle, camellia, or holly underplanted seasonally. In Japanese and Chinese gardens rocks and gravel are contrasted with gently clipped shrubs, which create a curvaceous outline that still flowers.

Holly, yew, and box

In 1925 Nathaniel Lloyd wrote *Garden Craftsmanship in Yew and Box*. In his own garden at Great Dixter in Sussex he planted yew hedges to mirror the roof lines of his old house, topped by a positive aviary of topiary peacocks. His son Christopher continues the tradition, infilling the great dark outlines of the garden with floral plantsmanship.

In her excellent book *Eminent Gardeners* Jane Brown writes of the parallel gardening styles, on different sides of the Atlantic, created by Harvey Ladew in Maryland and Lawrence Johnston in Gloucestershire. The Ladew Topiary Gardens include a full hunting scene in topiary, with hedges cut into swans and other conceits, while Hidcote Manor has high and low hedges in a more restrained manner, creating frames, stilts, pillars, and birds. There are no specific herb gardens at Great Dixter, Ladew Topiary Gardens, or Hidcote Manor but herbs are well represented in the plant chorus.

Yew clippings are now collected in order to extract taxol, used in the treatment of leukemia; box may be strong-smelling and narcotic but the leaves, bark, and wood are all used under medical supervision. Rabbits in need of a tonic will nibble a holly stick; medicinal hollies include the common holly (*Ilex aquifolium*) and Paraguay or maté tea (*I. paraguensis*). The Yaupon holly (*I. vomitaria*) has been used extensively in the re-created gardens of historic colonial Williamsburg in Virginia.

If you decide to create formality (and protection) with inner hedging, and space is at a premium, it is far better to trim the roots than try to cram them into too small a trench. After planting the hedging, compact the soil on the cultivated side in order to encourage the roots to grow away and leech the goodness from the path or grass.

Resting on your laurels

Unfortunately, you see more straggling, thin-trunked, dusty bay lollipops outside shops and restaurants than the aromatic shiny-leaved *objets d'art* that they can be. The first principle, which applies to topiarizing any bush or tree, is that a stout trunk is essential for the plant's health and looks. Select the main shoot to form the trunk but leave the side shoots on until it has established, gradually pruning the side shoots off as the bay grows. These side shoots are feeding and strengthening the trunk, and are essential, so resist the temptation to remove them for as long as possible; the heel left by the side shoot will soon be absorbed into the outline of the trunk.

The so-called "Versailles" box was designed for moving orange trees and other "exoticks" in and out of their orangeries for winter and summer. The elegant simplicity of the painted wood protects the plant from extremes of heat and moisture. Smaller versions show off clipped santolina, box, or lavender to excellent effect. (You do not have to repot, you can just drop a plant in while it is still in its plastic container, and top it up with gravel.)

If you plan to put the bay (or myrtle) in an exposed position it will be hardier if its trunk is covered, so opt for a cone, dome, or pyramid

shape. You can buy a large selection of different frames to fit over
young bushes, so if you want to be adventurous, start when the
plant is young. Remember that every leaf is photosynthesizing and,
therefore, feeding the bay or myrtle. The dormant season for
evergreens is late spring and mid-autumn, so these are the times
for planting or repotting and pruning.

Divine myrtle

If you want to create a garden with Classical roots, bay and myrtle will
provide the mythology and metamorphoses; myrtle alone will plot the
political past. In ancient Rome there were two old myrtles, one called
the Patrician and the other the Plebeian. The political fortunes of the
nobles as against those of the Plebeians could be judged, as each plant
flourished or languished. The pair at the Museum of Garden History
in London, clipped as sentinel pillars, have grown equally for the last
25 years. Such descriptions remind me of the flourishing garden of
a family friend who has just died. Myrtle Kingham — whose husband
rejoiced in the name of Basil — had a rosemary bush that grew past
the eaves of the tile-clad walls of their house.

The myrtle family is enormous, with 120 genera and 3,850 species
of trees and shrubs ranging from the mosquito-deterrent eucalpytus
to spices such as cloves and allspice, and fruits, including guava. The
ones commonly used for topiary and specimen shrubs are all varieties
of the sweet myrtle (*Myrtus communis*), which has double-flowering and
variegated forms. The leaves are aromatic, and the white flowers have
sparkling gold stamens appearing in late summer to early autumn.

M. c. 'Microphylla' and 'Microphylla Variegata' are ideal for mophead shapes as their leaves are tiny, shiny, and densely formed. *M. c.* 'Tarentina', introduced from Virginia to Europe by John Tradescant, has a compact habit suitable for smaller gardens and containers.

Decent standards

The head gardener at Goodnerstone Park in Kent has imaginatively trimmed all sorts of plants into standards – that is a long primary stem or trunk with a rounded top. If you have a leggy santolina, lavender, or rosemary, make a virtue of it by putting in a supporting cane and training it into a standard. The more tender lemon verbena looks and smells great when trained, its trunk almost white with frills of new green leaf growth, and a floppy mophead of lemon-scented leaves.

If space is at a premium, or you want to have a range of varieties, both wisteria and honeysuckle can be trained into standards; this requires skill, so if you can afford it buy a ready formed one. Standard roses are routinely sold at heights of 1.2m (4ft) but, if you are prepared to wait, you can order the climbing or rambling roses (for weeping standards) to be budded at 1.8m (6ft) so that you have painterly rose trees like Claude Monet at Giverny.

At Little Moreton Hall in Cheshire the yew-enclosed garden within the moat is north facing but there is a delightful display of standard gooseberries underplanted with paeonies and hyssop. The Philadelphia Flower Show, held annually in March, attracts magnificent topiary entries. The small-leaved myrtle is one of most popular exhibits, formed into enormous globes or series of globes up a stout central trunk. One year there was a rosemary cut into an abstract form – styled around a central trunk, the side branches had been trained into asymmetrical blocks.

Ground globes

Many of the small woody herbs will clip into delightful soft globes. A volunteer at the Museum of Garden History in London does a superb topiary job, creating a sense of bringing plantings in and out of focus – not just the centrepiece estrade or cakestand variegated holly but also the seats gently edged with "sofa backs" of clipped germander, rosemary, or euonymus. My favourite at the Museum is the clipped globe of winter savory, which would do equally well in an attractive pot. Thymes such as the orange-scented *Thymus* x *citriodorus* 'Fragrantissimus' and the softer *T. vulgaris* 'Silver Posy' shape up well in the ground or in pots.

Framework

Ivy will rapidly swathe around any frame in green, green and white, or, green and gold, depending on the variety. Because of its clinging nature it lends itself to be trained into curvaceous and active shapes. Children visiting the conservatory at Longwood Gardens in Pennsylvania are greeted by a large ivy rabbit before they enter their own specially devised garden. And at the Michigan 4H Children's Garden there are huge ivy teddy bears. At Waddesdon Manor in Buckinghamshire the inner courtyard wall is decorated with a diaper or diamond pattern in ivy. The framework was put up in bamboo canes and then the ivy trained around it, ensuring that the straight edges were maintained and the effect was formal and architectural.

Tell Me a Story

Whether this book is armchair or bedtime reading, fantasy is as important in design as your arcane appreciation of the plants. All plants were believed to carry a signature, which indicated how they could be used to cure or enliven you, much of which has already been mentioned. Many plants stem from gods and nymphs who were metamorphosed – stories enhanced by the sight of the barren winter earth gradually sprouting miraculous flowers and fodder in the spring.

Children's stories and books are full of wonder plants. Recently The Enormous Caterpillar garden was designed at Weeting School in Norfolk, and it creates the shapes and colours in flowers of all the good things the caterpillar ate to become a beautiful butterfly. The Michigan 4H Children's Garden is packed not with make-believe but make-alive stories. They have butterfly-shaped beds filled with attractant flowers. Beatrix Potter's Peter Rabbit (in stone) nibbles a radish by the gate he squeezed under to get into Mr McGregor's garden, surrounded by his mother's "rabbit tobacco" – lavender, and the chamomile she gave to him to recover from his flight from the enraged Mr McGregor. A rainbow garden arcs with a range of flowers, vegetables, and herbs.

Many Shakespeare gardens have been created around the world, furnished by his frequent use of trees, flowers, and herbs to dress and set his dramatic scenes realistically and symbolically. Rosemary for remembrance, plus hot lavender, mints, savory, marjoram, and many more. Who could resist the midsummer offer of "Sleep thou, and I will wind thee in my arms, So doth the woodbine the sweet honeysuckle gently entwist?" He used mandrake for dastardly purposes but the more melodious mandragora for gentle sleep: in *Romeo and Juliet,* "And shrieks like mandrakes torn out of the earth, That living mortals hearing them run mad" but in *Antony and Cleopatra* "Give me to drink mandragora…That I may sleep out this great gap of time. My Antony is away". The root of the mandrake (*Mandragora officinarum*) has an almost human shape, and it was believed that it screamed when pulled from the ground. Under no circumstances should you hear the

screams as they were fatal, so you covered your ears and used a dog,
later destroyed, to pull out the root. Extracts are still used in the
preliminaries before general anesthetic. More recently, there is a
delightful scene when Harry Potter and Hermione are potting on
obstreperous baby mandrakes. They are interesting-looking plants
that form green seeds the size of golf balls under their floppy leaves.

The blue cowled flowers and poisonous potential of monkshood
(*Aconitum napellus*) are echoed in its many names: helmet flower,
friar's-cap, soldier's cap, turk's-cap, bear's foot, or garden wolfsbane.
There are about 100 species with blue, purple, pink, or white flowers
to suit most zones. They are an attractive herbal addition to the
summer and autumn border, and make frequent appearances in the
books of the detective writers Agatha Christie and Ellis Peters. The
Roman naturalist Pliny wrote: "Aconite alone, if there were nothing
else, … we know there is no poison in the world so quick in operation
as it, insomuch as if the shape or nature of any living creature of female
sex be touched therewith, it will not live after it one day to an end."

The story of Christmas roses (*Helleborus niger*), like the genesis of
so many plants, began in the fields around Bethlehem. On the night
on which Jesus was born a young girl, Madelon, peeped into the
stable but dared not go in because she had no present. She turned
away crying, and as her tears fell to the earth the Christmas rose
blossomed, providing her with a posy to take to the manger's side.

Many gardener's tales are zestier than fisherman's. You can paint a
garden canvas with cuttings taken (never pinched!) or plants bought
or given to you that will evoke lasting memories.

Directory of Herbs

Herbs range from ground-hugging carpets to evergreen trees that clothe your environs with subtle shades and sweet scents. Here, in alphabetical order, are brief descriptions of my personal shortlist of must-have herbs, gleaned from a worldwide tour of taste and style.

Achillea millefolium 'Moonlight' (Yarrow)

Anethum graveolens (Dill seedhead)

Achillea millefolium
(Yarrow, milfoil)
Spreading mat of fern-like leaves with long stems of flower clusters; traditional stauncher of blood; many cultivars from 'White Beauty' to cream 'Moonlight' to pink-purple 'Purpureum'. Very hardy, can be invasive but good decorative border herb. Lighter shades good for evening gardens.
Height: 10–100cm+ (4in–3ft+)
Hardiness: Frost hardy

Aconitum napellus
(Aconite, monkshood, wolfsbane)
Poisonous tuberous roots, upright leafy stems with hooded flowers; invaluable in late-summer border; blue-, white-, and purple-flowering forms; many attractive cultivars.
Height: 1.2–1.5m (4–5ft)
Hardiness: Frost hardy

Aegopodium podagraria
(Ground elder, goutweed)
Invasive rhizomes difficult to eradicate; eat leaves like spinach before summer flowering. *A. p.* 'Variegatum' (Variegated ground elder), cream-splashed variegated form excellent weed smotherer.
Height: 90cm (3ft)
Hardiness: Frost hardy

Agastache foeniculum
(Anise hyssop)
Perennial with pointed aromatic aniseed-scented ovate leaves, flowerhead long lasting with hyssop-like flowers; rich source of nectar for bees; *A. f.* 'Alabaster' has white flowerheads; *A. rugosa* (Korean mint) hardier with mint scent.
Height: 60–90cm (24–36in)
Hardiness: Half-hardy

Alcea rosea
(Hollyhock)
Tall, short-lived, summer flowering perennial, stalwart of cottage gardens; roots formerly candied to make marshmallows; many colour forms *A. r.* 'Nigra' has almost black flowers.
Height: 1–2.5m (3–8ft)
Hardiness: Frost hardy

Alchemilla mollis
(Lady's mantle)
Robust perennial with clouds of pale lemon flowers above downy palmate leaves; colonizes dry and inhospitable conditions; true medicinal form is *A. xanthochlora*; *A. alpina* (alpine lady's mantle) is a smaller form with delicate white marginal variegation to leaves.
Height: 10–30cm (4–12in)
Hardiness: Frost hardy

Allium spp.
Onion family includes herbs such as chives and garlic, as well as many ornamentals; *A. sativum* (garlic), globose bulb of 5–15 cloves; plant single cloves to form bulbs: *A. schoenoprasum* (chives) *A. s.* 'Alba' (white-flowering chives), or *A. s.* 'Forescate' (pink-flowering), clump forming with slender onion-scented spikes; cut clump back immediately after flowering, flowers edible; *A. tuberosum* (garlic or Chinese chives), stout rhizome with flat leaves, garlic tasting, white flowers edible;

A. ursinum (Ramsons garlic) white-flowered carpeting perennial with strong garlic scent for woodland and wild gardens, very floriferous in spring.
Height: 20–50cm (9–19in)
Hardiness: Frost hardy

Aloysia triphylla
(Lemon verbena)
Tender small deciduous tree; sharp, clear, warm lemon scent from leaves and bark; can be trained as topiary; panicles of tiny, pale lilac flowers in hot summers. Same conditions as chaste tree (*Vitex*).
Height: 1–3m (3–10ft)
Hardiness: Tender

Anethum graveolens
(Dill)
Annual culinary herb; typically one stem rises to large yellow umbel, leaves as with fennel but smoky parsley taste; leaves and seeds both excellent with food; cultivar 'Dukat' good for leaves and 'Mammoth' for seeds; decorative in borders.
Height: 60–90cm (24–35in)
Hardiness: Hardy annual

Angelica archangelica
(Angelica)
Robust short-lived perennial with large globular seed head; "jungle" herb with dramatic foliage interest; raise from fresh seed; young leaves in salads, stems for candying.
Height: 1–2.5m (3–8ft)
Hardiness: Frost hardy

Anthriscus cerefolium
(Chervil)
Self-seeding annual with bright green parsley-like leaves, aniseed flavour, one of *fines herbes*; excellent catch crop in edible landscaping.
Height: 30–60cm (12–24in),
Hardiness: Hardy annual

Armoracia rusticana
(Horseradish)
Fleshy taproots regenerate prolifically; prepare 15–20cm pencil thick "thongs" in winter, store in cool, plant out in spring, lift in autumn for good-sized cooking roots; more ornamental *A. r.* 'Variegata' (variegated horseradish) has cream or white splashed leaves.
Height: 50cm–1m (2–3ft)
Hardiness: Frost hardy

Artemisia spp.
(Wormwood)
A. absinthium (wormwood) subshrub with grey-green, deeply dissected foliage; ornamental forms include *A. a.* 'Lambrook Silver' and 'Powys Castle'; *A. a. arborescens* with delicate, narrow, silver-white leaves; *A. schmidana nana* is a dwarf finely-cut silver leaves; *A. ludoviciana* (white sage) and whiter form *A. l. latifolia*; *A. abrotanum* (southernwood, maiden's ruin, old man) hardy hedging herb, moth repellent; *A. dracunculus* (French tarragon not *A. d.* ssp. *dracunculoides*, which is Russian tarragon), upright branched aromatic stems, smooth leaves with smoky aniseed flavour; needs warm well-drained site.
Height: 8cm–1m (3in–3ft)
Hardiness: Frost hardy

Borago officinalis 'Alba' (White flowering borage)

Chamaemelum nobile 'Flore Pleno' (Double-flowering camomile)

Atriplex hortensis
(Orache)
Fast-growing, self seeding annual, upright with heart-shaped leaves, saline tolerant so good for marine situations; eat when young then leave as ornamental colour; *A. h.* 'Rubra' (red orache) gives good colour tones to borders.
Height: 60cm–1m (2–3ft)
Hardiness: Hardy annual

Borago officinalis
(Borage)
Hairy annual with upright, hollow stems and blue five-petalled star flowers, self seeding; use leaves in drinks, flowers edible; *B. o.* 'Alba' (white flowering borage).
Height: 30cm–1m (1ft–3ft)
Hardiness: Hardy annual

Buxus sempervirens
(Common box)
Evergreen, hardy, hedging plant; invaluable element in formal gardening and topiary; suitable for supervised medicinal uses.
B. s. 'Suffruticosa' (dwarf box) for intricate and low hedging.
Height: 30cm–5m (1ft–16ft)
Hardiness: Frost hardy

Calamintha nepeta
(Calamint)
Bushy perennial with peppermint-scented catmint-shaped leaves and clusters of tubular mauve and white flowers; drought tolerant, free flowering and self-seeding; useful instant landscaper.
Height: 20–75cm (8–30in)
Hardiness: Frost hardy

Calendula officinalis
(Marigold)
Long-lived annual, lanceolate leaves and orange daisy flowers, single and double forms; self seeds and best planted in groups; petals in salads and soups; beneficial insect attractant plant; not to be mistaken for Tagetes marigolds.
Height: 30–60cm (1–2ft)
Hardiness: Hardy annual

Capsicum annuum
(Sweet or chilli pepper)
Many varieties from sweetly crisp to fiery hot; good in ground or pots; attractive addition under glass or in areas with hot summers for kitchen gardens; spice extracts include paprika, cayenne pepper, and chilli powder.
Height: 30–90cm (1–3ft)
Hardiness: Tender annual

Carum carvi
(Caraway)
Biennial umbellifer, leaves have faint characteristic smell of the seeds; sow in combination with coriander but leave to harvest seeds the following year; attractive feathery leaves.
Height: 25–90CM (10–36in)
Hardiness: Hardy biennial

Chamaemelum nobile
(Lawn chamomile)
Creeping perennial with apple scented leaves and daisy flowers; *C. n.* 'Flore Pleno' (double-flowering chamomile) more compact form with double flowers; *C. n.* 'Treneague' non-flowering form;

flowers used in tisanes; better sat on than walked across.
Height: 2.5–15cm (1–6in)
Hardiness: Frost hardy

Cimicifuga racemosa
(Black cohosh, Bugbane)
Perennial with knotty black rhizome; tall white fragrant flower spires may need staking; native of woodland needs moist, preferably acidic, soil.
Height: 1.5m (5ft)
Hardiness: Frost hardy

Coriandrum sativum
(Coriander, Cilantro)
Pungently aromatic leaf and seed; attractive finely-dissected leaves; sow successively, runs rapidly to seed – do not use seeds until ripe and papery.
Height: 30–60cm (1–2ft)
Hardiness: Hardy annual

Daphne mezereum
(Mezereon, February daphne)
Short-lived deciduous shrub growing, red or white flowers precede leaves in winter; *Daphne bholua* evergreen or deciduous shrub, heavily scented white to purple pink flowers in winter; *Daphne genkwa* sparsely-branched deciduous shrub growing to 1m (3ft), flower buds used in Chinese medicine.
Height: 1–4m (3–14ft)
Hardiness: Frost hardy

Dendranthema coronarium
(Garland chrysanthemum)
Chinese tong ho, Japanese kog-niku, annual with spicy foliage and yellow flowers; leaves form part of chop-suey greens; harvest leaves six weeks after sowing.
Height: 10–12cm (4–5in)
Hardiness: Hardy annual

Dianthus carophyllus
(Clove pink, Carnation, Gillyflower)
Perennial with glaucous silver spiky foliage and clove-scented flowers; flowers can be pure pink, red, white, or yellow, or striped; traditionally floated in wine cups; essential for scented gardens; hundreds of varieties, so ensure you choose one with scent. *D. chinensis* and *D. superbus* used medicinally. Carnation is the national flower of Portugal.
Height: 20–60cm (8–24in)
Hardiness: Frost hardy

Digitalis purpurea, D. lanata
(Foxglove)
Both used to extract digitoxin; spikes of veined flowers ranging from cream to purple, making attractive border plants; sun or partial shade; many ornamental cultivars available.
Height: 60cm–1m (2–3ft)
Hardiness: Frost hardy

Echinacea purpurea
(Purple coneflower)
Short-lived, tall perennial; native of North America, used in medicine; honey-scented petals radiate from central cone; colourful display from midsummer to early autumn; *E. pallida* has white flowers.
Height: 1.2m (4ft)
Hardiness: Frost hardy

Cimicifuga racemosa (Bugbane)

Echinacea purpurea (Purple coneflower)

Eruca vesicaria *ssp.* sativa
(Salad rocket, Arugola, Rucola)
Annual salading herb with oak-shaped leaves and fragrant, nutty four-petalled cream flowers; sow successively; appears to grow best early or later in the year.
Height: 20–45cm (8–18in)
Hardiness: Hardy annual

Eryngium foetidum
(Culantro, Fitweed, False coriander)
Perennial branching aromatic, native to Central America and Florida; numerous green-white spiky flowers. Note also Vietnamese coriander, *Polygonum odoratum*. *E. maritimum*, sea holly, traditional northern European source of candied eryngo, many ornamental cultivars.
Height: 60–90cm (24–35in)
Hardiness: Tender to frost hardy

Euonymus *spp.*
(Spindle family)
Mostly grown for their foliage; *E. europaeus* (spindle tree) traditional woodland tree with distinctive pink fruits; *E. japonicus* more tender substitute for box, best clipped, many varieties of leaf colour and variegation; N. American *E. atropurpureus* (wahoo, burning bush, Indian arrow-wood) used medicinally.
Height: 2–7m (6¹⁄₂–23ft)
Hardiness: Frost hardy

Euphorbia *spp.*
(Spurge)
Toxic and irritant milky-white sap; conspicuously coloured and long-lasting bracts; *E. lathyris* (caper spurge, myrtle spurge, mole plant) reputedly deters moles; *E. characias* ssp. *wulfenii*, and other cultivars, especially ornamental; excellent in borders with heads in sunshine.
Height: 1.5–2m (5–6½ft)
Hardiness: Frost hardy

Ficus carica
(Fig)
Records show cultivation in 2,700 BC for this ancient fruit tree; essential to restrict roots to ensure good fruiting; excellent food and medicine fresh and dried; needs south-east, south, or west-facing wall for fruit to ripen; good subject for pot culture; underplant with rue.
Height: 2–5m (6¹⁄₂–16FT)
Hardiness: Frost hardy

Filipendula ulmaria
(Meadowsweet, Queen of the meadow)
Native of damp meadows and ditches; creamy scented flower plumes; the aspirin base of salicylic acid first isolated in 1838; planting under the medlar tree is believed to ward off evil; ornamental cultivars available.
Height: 60–100cm (2–3ft)
Hardiness: Frost hardy

Foeniculum vulgare
(Fennel)
Sweet, aromatic, aniseed-tasting perennial herb; long stems and yellow umbels; traditional accompaniment for fish, good in salads; seeds suppress appetite; *F. v.* 'Purpureum' (bronze fennel) as sweet fennel, feathery leaves almost black when young, growing to bronze purple. Cross pollinates so separate from other umbellifers.
Height: 2m (6½ft)
Hardiness: Frost hardy

Galega officinalis
(Goat's rue)
Native of damp meadows, ditches, and riverbanks of Europe; vigorous herbaceous perennial for late-summer borders with slender flower spikes; reputedly raises milk yields in cows and goats; many attractive cultivars such as 'Lady Wilson' with lilac-blue spikes; pre-soak seeds for 12 hours before sowing.
Height: 60–100cm (24–35in)
Hardiness: Frost hardy

Galium odoratum
(Sweet woodruff)
Perennial in the bedstraw family; good groundcover with mass of white starry flowers in late spring; contains coumarin so valuable fixative when mixed with dry herbs; thrives in shade; add to wine cups.
Height: 30cm (1ft)
Hardiness: Frost hardy

Ginkgo biloba
(Maidenhair tree, Chinese yin-kuo)
Fossil evidence dating back 200 million years; leaves shaped like maidenhair fern; extracts widely available to promote mental alertness; male clones best for gardens, as fruit malodorous; needs sunny position.
Height: 4–8m, (13–25ft)
Hardiness: Frost hardy

Hamamelis *spp.*
(Witch hazel)
Small trees prized for their winter blossom and medicinal wash; need moist, neutral to acidic soil; *H. mollis* (Chinese witch hazel) sweetly fragrant yellow flowers in late winter to early spring; *H. virginiana* (Virginian witch hazel) distilled extract from leaves, branches, and bark used externally as an astringent.
Height: 3–5m (9–15ft)
Hardiness: Frost hardy

Hedera helix
(Ivy)
Eleven species of evergreen, woody, climbing or creeping plants; valued for covering walls, sheds, tree stumps, and for training over iron frames for topiary; *H. h.* 'Sagittifolia variegata' with variegated arrow shaped leaves; symbol of steadfastness.
Height: 60cm+ (2ft+)
Hardiness: Frost hardy

Helichrysum italicum
(Curry plant, Everlasting flower)
Silver-white tomentose leaves with distinctive curry scent; subshrub for massed planting; cut back to base each spring; good foil for purple-leaved herbs in night garden; dwarf form also available.
Height: 45–60cm (18in–24in)
Hardiness: Frost hardy

Ginkgo biloba (Maidenhair tree)

Iris germanica var. *florentina* (Orris root iris)

Hesperis matronalis
(Sweet rocket, Dames' rocket)
Biennial that self-seeds; mauve- and white-flowering forms; colour and fragrance excellent for evening garden; general nectar source for butterflies, and food source for the caterpillars of the orange-tip butterfly; frequent garden escape.
Height: 60–90cm (24–35in)
Hardiness: Frost hardy

Hypericum perforatum
(St John's wort)
Creeping yellow-flowered herb; leaves perforated with tiny glands – both they and the flowers yield a red oil; will colonize gravel and dry soils.
Height: 30–60cm (1–2ft)
Hardiness: Frost hardy

Hyssopus officinalis
(Hyssop)
Perennial hedging herb; needs cutting back to base each spring; flowers white, pink, blue, and purple, attractive to bees; *H. aristatus* (rock hyssop) dwarf form for edging and rockeries; use leaves in *herbes provençales.*
Height: 30–60cm (1–2ft)
Hardiness: Frost hardy

Inula helenium
(Elecampane)
Thrives in damp or moisture-retentive soil; flat, shaggy yellow daisy flowers and downy pale green foliage; good for borders; formerly a culinary now medicinal herb; also a good range of low-growing species for rock gardens.
Height: 1–1.5m (3–5ft)
Hardiness: Frost hardy

Iris germanica *var.* florentina
(Orris root)
Pale blue, almost white flowering iris; sword-shaped leaves and elegant flowerheads rising to 60–100cm (2–3ft); rhizomes dried for orris root powder; likes well-drained sunny position; also elegant *I. unguicularis* for winter scent; dwarf *I. reticulata* for spring scent.
Height: 60cm–1.2m (2–4ft)
Hardiness: Frost hardy

Isatis tinctoria
(Woad)
Biennial famously associated with the blue-painted Boudicca and Ancient Britons; stout tap root, tall branching stems topped with massed yellow, four-petalled flowers; dye plant; good border plant; self-seeds.
Height: 50cm–1.2m (19in–4ft)
Hardiness: Frost hardy

Jasminum officinale
(Common jasmine, Jessamine)
Wall climbing and free-standing shrubs grown for their heavily fragrant flowers; white flowers in summer; also *J. nudiflorum* (winter flowering jasmine) yellow flowers, good soil stabilizer on banks, very hardy – both will take hard clipping; *J. sambac* tender, highly scented white flowers, good for indoor or conservatory pots.
Height: 1.5m–3m (5–10ft)
Hardiness: Frost hardy

Juniperus communis
(Juniper)
Densely branching shrub or tree; fruits or berries used to flavour food and gin; important medicinal uses; berries should only be eaten in small quantities.
Height: 2–10m (6½–33ft)
Hardiness: Frost hardy

Lavandula *spp.*
(Lavender)
Genus of 21 grey-green to silver subshrubs; dwarf *L. angustifolia* 'Nana alba' to giant lavenders *L.* x *allardii*; globular formed *L.* x *intermedia* 'Grosso'; spike flowerheads in purple, white or pink; excellent for fragrant hedges or for massed planting on slopes, always prune to a bud; use leaves in cooking.
Height: 15–1.5m (6in–5ft)
Hardiness: Tender to frost hardy

Levisticum officinale
(Lovage)
Tall "jungle" perennial; smooth divided leaves with strong celery flavour; young leaves excellent in salads; indistinct flower clusters in summer; will self-seed; grows well with angelica.
Height: 1–2m (3–6½ft)
Hardiness: Frost hardy

Laurus nobilis
(Sweet bay, Bay laurel)
Evergreen shrub or small tree ornamental and culinary herb; tolerates clipping and excellent for large tubs; *L. n.* 'Aureum' golden-leaved form; after winter if bay seems dead leave until late spring as often regenerates from base.
Height: 3–15m (10–50ft)
Hardiness: Frost hardy

Lilium candidum
(Madonna lily)
The traditional herb-garden lily, introduced throughout Europe by the Romans in their *materia medica*; prefers poor soil and shaded base, so ideal for growing through lavenders; huge range of scented and colourful lilies suitable for growing with herbs and in pots.
Height: 1–1.5m (3–5ft)
Hardiness: Frost hardy

Lonicera *spp.*
(Honeysuckle, Woodbine)
Enormous range of hardy shrubs and climbers flowering for every season; the shrub *L. fragrantissima* has orange flower scent from tiny winter flowers; the climbers include early Dutch *L. belgica* and later *L. serotina*; *L.* 'Graham Stuart Thomas' has creamy-yellow flowers and a superb orange flower scent; climbing forms can be trained over trellises, arbours, and into standards.
Height: 1.5–3m (5–10ft)
Hardiness: Frost hardy

Mandragora officinarum
(Mandrake)
A wide rosette of wrinkled, malodorous leaves shelter short stalked flowers, followed by aromatic deep yellow poisonous fruits that ripen green; packed with terrifying folklore; best avoided if you have children.
Height: 20–30cm (8–12in)
Hardiness: Frost hardy

Mandragora officinarum (Mandrake)

Myrrhis odorata (Sweet cicely)

Marrubium vulgare
(White horehound)
An undistinguished downy herb with tiny white flowers in whorls around the stem; interesting when used for contrasting texture and for its medicinal history; cough remedy for ancient Egyptians; prefers dry sunny site.
Height: 20–60cm (8–24in)
Hardiness: Frost hardy

Melilotus officinalis
(Melilot)
Useful "jungle" herb as it self-seeds prodigiously; pea-like leaves and flowers; fixes nitrogen in soil; contains coumarins so useful fixative for dried herb mixtures.
Height: 90–120cm (3–4ft)
Hardiness: Frost hardy

Melissa officinalis
(Lemon balm)
Vigorous herb in the mint family; lemon scented; young leaves excellent in salads and teas, good for mind and body; *M. o.* 'All Gold' (Golden lemon balm) attractive and slightly less vigorous variety; good edging or starter herb but do not allow it to go to seed as it will rapidly become a thug.
Height: 30–80cm (12–31in)
Hardiness: Frost hardy

Mentha *spp.*
(Mint)
Wide range of vigorous herbs prized for food and medicine; *M. gracilis* (gingermint, redmint); *M.* × *piperita* (peppermint); *M. crispa* (curled mint); *M. suaveolens* 'Variegata' (variegated applemint); do not eat low-growing fly and ant repellent *M. pulegium* (pennyroyal), or the diminutive *M. requenii* (Corsican mint); prefers moisture retentive soils.
Height: 1cm–1m (⅜in–3ft)
Hardiness: Frost hardy

Monarda fistulosa
(Bergamot, Bee balm)
Perennial herb, square stems, ovate leaves and whorls of shaggy flowers – red, white, or pink; prefers moisture retentive soil. *M. didyma* (Oswego tea), common name recalls its North American origins; good in tea or milk; smells like bergamot oranges; *M. citriodora* (lemon bergamot) is more tender.
Height: 35–1.2m (14in–47in)
Hardiness: Tender to frost hardy

Myrrhis odorata
(Sweet cicely)
Sweetly aromatic aniseed-scented perennial umbellifer; profusion of ferny foliage and creamy-white flowers; natural sweetener for rhubarb; use to fill early border and in dappled shade.
Height: 1–1.2m (3–4ft)
Hardiness: Frost hardy

Myrtus communis
(Sweet myrtle)
Evergreen shrub that thrives in sheltered garden; pink or white flowers with prominent golden stamens; spicy aromatic foliage; good for clipping and training; *M. c.* 'Flore Pleno' double flowering; *M. c.* 'Microphylla' tiny leaved; *M. c.* 'Tarentina' compact growth;

symbol of divine love and happy marriage.
Height: 1–3m (3–10ft)
Hardiness: Protect from frost

Nepeta cataria
(Catmint)
Nettle-like stems with massed pale-pink flowers; suitable for wilder garden; ornamental forms include *N.* × *faassenii* sterile and *N. racemosa* 'Superba' syn. *N. mussini* 'Superba'; attracts cats and deters mice; grey-green to silver foliage and mass of lavender-blue flowerheads; pink- and white-flowering forms; excellent for massed and hedge planting; attractive to bees.
Height: 30cm–1m (1–3ft)
Hardiness: Frost hardy

Nigella damascena
(Love-in-the-mist, Fennel flower)
Annual native of sub-alpine meadows; feathery foliage and long-lasting blue haze of summer flower; self seeding ideal for naturalizing even in formal plantings; *N. sativa* (black cumin, nutmeg flower, Roman coriander) less ornamental but pungently aromatic seeds.
Height: 20–50cm (8–19in)
Hardiness: Hardy annual

Nymphaea odorata
(White pond lily, Sweet-scented water lily)
Needs rich soil in still water up to 45cm (18in) deep; astringent, soothing herb; valuable addition to formal and informal ponds and pools; many varieties.
Height: spreads across water surface
Hardiness: Tender to frost hardy

Ocimum basilicum
(Basil)
Tender perennial requiring warm, well-drained conditions; raise from seed; varieties include *O. b.* 'Anise', *O. b.* 'Cinnamon', *O. b.* 'Dark Opal', *O. b.* 'Genovese', *O. b.* Mini purpurascens 'Wellsweep' (compact purple-leaved basil), *O. b.* 'Green Ruffles', *O. b.* 'Purple Ruffles', *O. b.* var. *citriodorum* (lemon scented basil), *O. b.* 'Lettuce Leaf', *O. sanctum* (holy basil); essential salad and culinary herb; good for pot culture.
Height: 20–100cm (8–36in)
Hardiness: Treat as tender annual

Oenothera biennis
(Evening primrose)
Self-seeding biennial; large, showy, pale yellow flowers; evening scented; much used medicinally for hormonal complaints; will naturalize; dwarf forms available.
Height: 60cm–1.5m (2–4ft)
Hardiness: Frost hardy

Origanum vulgare
(Marjoram, Oregano)
Perennial cushion-forming herb with aromatic scented leaves; mostly hardy with range of golden, green and variegated foliage; *O. v.* 'Album' with white flowers; *O. v.* 'Aureum' with golden leaves excellent for spring effect and informal hedging; *O. v.* 'Aureum Crispum' attractive crinkled golden leaves tidier than type; *O. v.* 'Compactum' tidy green mound with excellent flavour, lasts well into winter; *O. v.* 'Gold Tip' green leaves with attractive gold tips, excellent for edging; *O. majorana*

Myrtus communis (Sweet myrtle)

Pelargonium crispum 'Variegatum' (Lemon-scented geranium)

(sweet marjoram) more delicately scented and flavoured; *O. onites* (Greek oregano) thyme-like flavour; all excellent sweetly aromatic culinary herbs.
Height: 15–60cm (6in–2ft)
Hardiness: Frost hardy

Papaver somniferum
(Opium poppy)
Self-seeding pink-flowered annual; variable producing single and double flowers; allow to colonize; use seeds on bread and cakes; also attractive cultivars such as the Peony-flowered hybrids; *P. rhoeas* (corn poppy) bright red flowers for wild plantings; *P. orientale* (oriental poppy) herbaceous perennial with enormous ornamental flowers.
Height: 30cm–100cm (1–3ft)
Hardiness: Frost hardy

Pelargonium *spp.*
(Geranium)
Scented-leaved geraniums of herbal interest; lemon, rose, nutmeg, balsam, pine, apple scents; treat as tender, and pot plants possibly bed out in summer; leaf shapes from deeply dissected to round wavy-edged; flowers small, in shades of pink; *P. citronellum* (lemon scented); *P. crispum* and *P. c.* 'Variegatum' (variegated lemon-scented geranium); *P. odoratissimum* (apple scented); *P.* 'Graveolens' (rose scented).
Height: 30–150cm (1–5ft)
Hardiness: Tender

Perilla frutescens 'Crispa'
(Purple-leaved Japanese basil, Shiso)
Six species of aromatic annuals; culinary herb for raw fish and salads; excellent bedding plant with crinkled ornamental leaves.
Height: 60–120cm (2–4ft)
Hardiness: Treat as tender annual

Petroselinum crispum
(Parsley)
Aromatic culinary biennial with attractive curled leaves or plain-leaved form *P .c.* 'Italian'; essential for any herb or kitchen garden; unusual edging for borders; hardy, requires rich soil for good leaf production.
Height: 30–80cm (1–2ft 6in)
Hardiness: Frost hardy

Pimpinella anisum
(Anise)
True aniseed; aromatic dissected foliage, creamy-white umbels and ribbed seeds; requires more warmth than dill, fennel, or coriander; good for salad basket or leave as ornamental annual harvesting seed at season's end.
Height: 50cm (19in)
Hardiness: Tender annual

Plectranthus amboinicus
(Indian borage, Spanish thyme)
Aromatic tender perennial; treat as pot plant and bed out in summer; attractive thick square stems and succulent foliage.
Height: 30cm–1m (1–3ft)
Hardiness: Tender

Polygonatum odoratum
(Solomon's seal)
Poisonous perennial rhizome; arching stems with pendulous tubular flowers rising to attractive pointed foliage, variegated forms available; formerly used medicinally; thrives in dry shade.
Height: 80cm (31in)
Hardiness: Frost hardy

Polygonum bistorta
(Snakeweed, Bistort)
Double-twisted root has given rise to common name; hardy creeping perennial with mass of dense pink flower spikes; also tender *P. odoratum* (Vietnamese coriander, Rau ram, Japanese baday) lemon-coriander flavour.
Height: 25–50cm (9–19in)
Hardiness: Frost hardy

Portulaca oleracea
(Purslane)
Succulent annual salad herb; round leaves; rich source of omega-3 fatty acids; also *P. o.* 'Aurea' (Golden leaved purslane).
Height: 20–45cm (8–18in)
Hardiness: Tender annual

Pulmonaria officinalis
(Lungwort, Virgin Mary's Milkdrops, Soldiers and Sailors)
Hardy spreading perennial; speckled variegated leaves look like lungs; typically blue and red hanging flowers; many attractive cultivars; shade tolerant and good colonizer; modern cultivars include dark-blue flowered and elegantly spotted 'Beth Chatto', later flowering 'Mawson's Blue'.
Height: 10–30cm (4–12in)
Hardiness: Frost hardy

Ricinus communis
(Castor oil plant)
Dramatic red downy stems, palmate leaves, and globular flowerheads; tender; excellent for tropical schemes; seeds very poisonous.
Height: 1.5–2m (5–6½ft)
Hardiness: Treat as tender annual

Rosa *spp.*
(Rose)
There is a rose for every aspect and situation — bush, climbing, rambling, or standard; choose scented and fragrant varieties; traditional is apothecary's rose, *Rosa gallica officinalis*; use in scented, culinary, and symbolic schemes.
Height: 60cm–4m+ (2ft–12ft+)
Hardiness: Frost hardy

Rosmarinus officinalis
(Rosemary)
Evergreen aromatic perennial; native of Mediterranean region; excellent wall shrub up to 2m (6ft); silver variegated form 'Silver Spires' not very hardy; many shades of blue such as 'Sudbury Blue', also pink 'Majorca pink' and white 'Alba' flowering varieties; must be well drained, likes coastal conditions; excellent for health promotion, in cooking and for scent.
Height: 30cm–2m (1–6ft)
Hardiness: Frost hardy if well drained and sheltered

Rumex scutatus
(Buckler-leaf sorrel)
Mat-forming perennial, happy in shade; more delicate in growth and taste than the common large-leaved sorrel (*R. acetosa*);

Santolina chamaecyparissus (Cotton lavender)

Salvia viridis 'Clary' (Clary sage)

arrowhead-shaped leaves with sharp lemony taste; *R. s.* 'Silver Shield' is more ornamental with a white sheen; best treated as a short-lived perennial.
Height: 15–50cm (6–19in)
Hardiness: Frost hardy

Salvia *spp.*
(Sage family)
Large variety of hardy and tender, edible, medicinal, and ornamental herbs; the common green and purple sages (*S. officinalis* and *S. o.* Purpurascens) and their variegated forms are multi-purpose and excellent for any garden; the lavender-leaved sage (*S. lavandulifolia*) is more tomentose with mass of violet-blue flowers; the clary sages are annual and biennial with pink-, purple- or white-coloured bracts, varieties include *S. sclarea* var. *turkestanica*, and *S. viridis* 'Claryssa'; there are tender forms with fruit- (*S. dorisiana*) and pineapple- (*S. rutilans*) scented leaves and magenta or red flowers.
Height: 20–100cm (8in–3ft)
Hardiness: Tender to frost hardy

Sambucus nigra
(Elder, Elderberry)
Small versatile hardy trees tolerant of poor soils and shade; creamy-white muscat scented umbels followed by purple-black berries; flowers and berries excellent medicinal value; ornamental forms for smaller gardens include golden elder (*S. n.* 'Aurea'), bronze elder (*S. n.* 'Guincho Purple'), and cut-leaved elder (*S. racemosa* 'Plumosa'), or the double-pink-flowering *S. n.* 'Rosea-plena'.
Height: 1–10m (3–30ft)
Hardiness: Frost hardy

Sanguisorba officinalis
(Great Burnet, Burnet Bloodwort)
Herbaceous meadow perennial traditionally used to staunch blood; the lesser form Salad burnet (*S. minor*) is more ornamental, useful for mass planting and edging in a wide range of soils; characteristic red bottle brush flowerheads; young leaves good in salads.
Height: 45cm–1m (18in–3ft)
Hardiness: Frost hardy

Santolina *spp.*
(Cotton lavender)
Silver or green fine-leaved ornamental aromatic subshrub with mass of pompom daisy flowers; invaluable for edging and infilling; its name derives from the Latin *sanctum linum* – holy flax; drought tolerant; *S. chamaecyparissus* is the hardiest, including 'Lambrook Silver', 'Lemon Queen', and 'Pretty Carol'; *S. pinnata* ssp. *etrusca* has cream-yellow flowers and *S.p.* ssp. *neopolitana* is tall with elegant frondy leaves; *S. rosmarinifolia* has deep-green branches with bright yellow flowers; cut back hard in spring and deadhead in late summer.
Height: 30cm–1m (1–3ft)
Hardiness: Frost hardy

Saponaria officinalis
(Soapwort, Bouncing Bet)
As name suggests, roots and stems yield mild lather; vigorous perennial good for informal and naturalistic plantings in sun or light shade; the shaggy pale-pink

flowers are good in evening gardens; double-flowered *S. o.* 'Rosea Plena' and variegated forms more attractive.
Height: 30–60cm (1–2ft)
Hardiness: Hardy

Satureja montana
(Winter savory)
Hardy, spiky aromatic perennial herb with pale-pink flowers; can be trimmed into small globes; culinary leaves; thrives in dry, sunny position; summer savory, annual form, more aromatic, ideally grown alongside and eaten with beans.
Height: 15–30cm (6in–1ft)
Hardiness: Hardy

Stachys officinalis
(Betony, Bishopswort)
Mat-forming perennial with deeply veined dark-green leaves and magenta, pink, or white flowers for borders or naturalizing; the pubescent lamb's ears, *S. byzantina*, creates a white woolly-leaved edging along paths and other dry sunny spots; the marsh woundwort *S. palustris* makes an attractive bog plant.
Height: 30–60cm (1–2ft)
Hardiness: Hardy

Symphytum *spp.*
(Comfrey, Knitbone)
Vigorous, medicinal, ornamental herb and green manure; invasive but excellent for difficult locations; leaves rich in potash; flowers white, pink, blue, and purple; variegated-leaved forms such as *S. x uplandicum* 'Variegatum'; for groundcover *S. grandiflora* will colonize under hedges; *S. officinale*, flowers off-white, woolly leaved; attractive variegated form.
Height: 60cm–1.5m (2–5ft)
Hardiness: Hardy

Tagetes *spp.*
(French, African, or Mexican Marigold)
Annuals with bright brassy flowers and dissected leaves, not to be confused with *Calendula* spp.; have insecticidal properties so used as barrier plantings in tomatoes and potatoes, especially *T. minuta*; the Mexican, *T. lucida*, is also known as sweet mace; the French is *T. patula*, 'Rusty Red' has fragrant red flowers.
Height: 20cm–1m (8in–3ft)
Hardiness: Tender annual

Tanacetum *spp.*
(Tansy)
Wide range of uses in rock, alpine, and herb gardens, as well as borders and for naturalizing; in the daisy family; can use as vegetable rennet now many ornamental forms; herbs include costmary (*T. balsamita*), feverfew (*T. parthenium*), single- and double-flowered as well as golden leaved, and the common tansy (*T. vulgare*) and its curly-leaved form (*T. vulgare crispum*).
Height: 30–120cm (1–4ft)
Hardiness: Hardy

Teucrium chamaedrys
(Wall germander)
Almost evergreen edging and hedging plant with pink-purple flowers; benefits from regular trimming; many ornamental and variegated forms; very hardy; tolerates some shade.
Height: 30–50cm (1–2ft)
Hardiness: Hardy

Symphytum officinale (Comfrey)

Verbascum chaixii orientale (Nettle-leaved mullein)

Tropaeolum majus
(Nasturtium, Indian Cress)
Strong-growing annual with edible flowers and leaves; flowers many shades of red and yellow; will scramble over ground or up framework; the smaller form *T. minus* includes the white variegated leaved 'Alaska'; essential for edible gardening and brightening up schemes.
Height: 30cm+ (1ft+)
Hardiness: Hardy annual

Thymus spp.
(Thymes)
Key plants for sunny gardens, creeping, groundcover, and bush forming; aromatic leaves and massed tiny flowers in pink, mauve, white, and purple; leaves tiny and silver to golden, or silver variegated; thyme-, lemon-, and orange-scented leaves; new varieties every year; the smaller the leaves the hardier, the larger the leaves the better for salads and ornamentation. Shown to slow ageing process.
Height: 2–45cm (1–18in)
Hardiness: Frost hardy

Urtica dioica
(Stinging nettle)
Needs no description, often classed as a weed! Left to colonize a wild area will attract butterflies; steamed young leaves good to eat in spring.
Height: 1m+ (3ft+)
Hardiness: Hardy

Valeriana officinalis
(Common valerian, Garden heliotrope)
Not to be confused with red valerian (*Centranthus ruber*). Tall perennial whose massed dense clusters of pinky-white flowers are ideal for the back of the summer border; important "calming" herb included in many herbal medicines.
Height: 1.5m (5ft)
Hardiness: Hardy

Verbena officinalis
(Vervain)
Not to be confused with the tender-scented lemon verbena. Perennial medicinal herb that self-seeds vigorously, useful for leaf interest early in season. Good range of more ornamental forms of *Verbena*.
Height: 80cm (31in)
Hardiness: Hardy

Verbascum thapsus
(Mullein, Aaron's rod)
Well-distributed family of annuals, biennials, and perennials. Tall erect yellow spires of flowers on woolly white stems give architectural accents in plantings; tolerant of dry, stony conditions; nettle-leaved mulleins *V. chaixii orientale* are notably floriferous; many ornamental cultivars for all zones.
Height: 1–1.8m (3–6ft)
Hardiness: Tender to hardy

Vinca minor
(Periwinkle)
Very hardy robust almost evergreen trailing groundcover plant; single or double blue or white flowers; variegated and darker-leaved varieties available; excellent for shady and difficult areas; larger-leaved form *V. major*. Not to be confused with the tender Madagascan periwinkle (*Catharanthus roseus*).
Height: 10–20cm (4–8in)
Hardiness: Hardy

Viola odorata
(Sweet violet)
Delightful creeping flower that colonizes shady, dry places; good under arbours, hedges, or in shady pockets; the 'Princess of Wales' is very fragrant, as is the white-flowering form; flowers can be eaten in salads; scent only available on first inhalation.
Height: 5cm+ (2in+)
Hardiness: Hardy

Vitex agnus-castus
(Chaste tree)
Deciduous, aromatic shrub or small tree with aromatic palmate leaves and spikes of small-scented lilac- or lavender-coloured, tubular flowers; needs sheltered warm placement and protection from cold winds. Same conditions as lemon verbena (*Aloysia triphylla*).
Height: 1–5m (3–16ft)
Hardiness: Tender

Vitis vinifera
(Vine, Grapevine)
Well-known climber with edible leaves and autumn clusters of grapes; many fruiting and ornamental varieties that can be trained over trellis, frames, and in pots. Always prune hard early in year to avoid sap loss.
Height: 2m+ (6½in+)
Hardiness: Hardy

Wisteria spp.
(Wisteria, Glycine)
Vigorous elegant climbers with attractive foliage and pendulous racemes of (mostly) scented flowers; flower colours range from white through mauves to dark purple; trained to cover large wall expanses, treillage, or as standards. Prefer a sunny south or southwest aspect. Prune close to plants framework to encourage fruiting spurs. Can be forced in pots.
Height: 2–8m (6''–26ft)
Hardiness: Hardy

Yucca spp.
Impressive strap-like leaves with spiny tips give a strong outline and handsome architectural form in sheltered gardens; the densely flowered spikes of pendent, tulip-shaped blooms make a dramatic show and exude scent in the evening garden. In well-drained conditions and protection from cold winds the hardiest are *Y. recurvifolia*, *Y. filamentosa*, *Y. glauca*, and *Y. gloriosa*, some with variegated leaved forms.
Height: Leaves 60–120cm (2–4ft); flowers up to 4.5m (15ft)
Hardiness: Hardy if well drained

Gardens To Visit

The locations listed have gardens where herbs have been used imaginatively in their plantings, although not necessarily herb gardens. The list is personal, and in direct relation with this book.

ENGLAND
The Alnwick Garden
Denwick Lane
Alnwick
Northumberland NE66 1YU
www.alnwickgarden.com
Grand-scale (walled) gardens to inspire – herbs with roses, flowers, fruit, and poison plants.

Capel Manor Gardens
Bullsmoor Lane
Enfield
Middlesex EN1 4RQ
Tel: (0)1992 716128
Some 30 acres of historical and modern-theme gardens, model and trial gardens. Good range of courses. Nursery.

Chatsworth
Bakewell
Derbyshire DE4 1PP
www.chatsworth-house.co.uk
Glorious park and gardens with historic and modern plantings, and sculpture. Kitchen garden. Nursery.

Chelsea Physic Garden
66, Royal Hospital Road
London SW3 4HS
www.EnglishGardening School.co.uk
Founded in 1673, this is a garden for study and leisure. Garden of World Medicine. Location for English Gardening School – courses in garden design and history.

Clinton Lodge
Fletching
Uckfield
Sussex
Tel: (0)1825 722952
A 2.5-ha (6-acre) formal and romantic garden. 17th-scented herb garden, medieval potager, old roses, wild-flower garden. Plants for sale.

Clock House
Coleshill
Faringdon
Oxfordshire
Tel: (0)1973 762476
Ground plan of old Coleshill House picked out in lavender and box with self-sown butterfly attractants.

Congham Hall Hotel
Lynn Road, Grimston
King's Lynn
Norfolk PE32 1AH
www.conghamhallhotel.co.uk
Hotel and restaurant with extensive and well-used herb garden. Edible landscaping at its absolute best.

Coton Manor
Guilsborough
Northamptonshire NN6 8RQ
www.cotonmanor.co.uk
Superb voluptuous plantings in extensive gardens. Specialist herb garden. Excellent nursery. Courses.

Cottesbrooke Hall
Cottesbrooke
Northamptonshire NN6 8PF
www.cottesbrookehall.co.uk
Immaculate, imaginative garden around a magnificent Queen Anne Hall. West and East wild gardens newly created. Sculpture.

Coughton Court
Alcester
Warwickshire B49 5JA
www.nationaltrust.org.uk
Historic house with new gardens. Walled garden with series of rooms and styles. Gardens use herbs and plants imaginatively. Nursery.

Denmans
Fontwell
Arundel
West Sussex BN18 0SU
www.denmans-garden.co.uk
Designer John Brookes has developed Mrs J.H. Robinson's original gardens. Curvaceous and imaginative. Nursery.

East Ruston Old Vicarage
East Ruston
Norfolk NR12 9HN
www.e-ruston-oldvicaragegardens.co.uk
Stunning series of gardens created since 1988. Plantsman and designer colour. Good nursery, plants raised on site.

Eltham Palace
Eltham
London SE9 5QE
www.english-heritage.org.uk
Art Deco restored and modern planting schemes. Groovy grids by Palace. One of a series of English Heritage modern design gardens in old settings.

Felley Priory
Jacksdale
Nottinghamshire NG16 5FL
Tel: 01773 810230
Sloping site on Nottinghamshire/Derbyshire borders. Created since 1980s. Plantsmanship and style. Good nursery from own stock.

Geffrye Museum
Kingsland Road
London E2 8EA
www.geffrye-museum.org.uk
Museum of Domestic Interiors
with good herb garden.
Historic themed gardens in
the making.

Hadspen Gardens
Castle Cary
Somerset BA7 7NG
Tel: (0)1749 813707
Colourful and imaginative,
with utility and beauty
newly interpreted.
Good nursery.

Hannah Peschar
Sculpture Garden
Black & White Cottage
Standon Lane,
Ockley, Surrey RH5 5QR
www.hannahpescharsculpture.com
A 4-ha (10-acre) garden with
exotic and naturalized planting
in a wooded valley with
running water. Designed
landscape and presentation
of works of art.

Hardwick Hall
Doe Lea
Chesterfield
Derbyshire S44 5QJ
www.nationaltrust.org.uk
Elizabethan prodigy house
with extensive herb garden.
Traditional but clever
use of tripods to
give height.

Hatfield House
Hatfield
Hertfordshire AL9 5NQ
www.hatfield-house.co.uk
Historically-inspired gardens
planted effectively with herbs.
Good traditional ideas for
all gardens.

Helmingham Hall
Helmingham
Stowmarket
Suffolk IP14 6EF
www.helmingham.com
Herbs used extensively in knot,
heraldic, and rose gardens.
Walled kitchen garden, walls,
and walks are planted
ornamentally. Plants and
produce for sale.

HDRA Ryton Organic Gardens
Ryton on Dunsmore
Coventry CV8 3LG
www.hdra.org.uk
Headquarters of HDRA the
Organic Organisation. Stylish
displays for every-sized garden.
New Vegetable Kingdom.
Nursery.

HDRA Yalding Organic Gardens
Benover Road, Yalding
Maidstone , Kent ME18 6EX
www.hdra.org.uk
Green chronology of gardens
designed by author. Superb
salad, vegetable, and fruit
display gardens. Nursery.

The Herb Garden
Hall View Cottage, Hardstoft
Pilsley, Chesterfield
Derbyshire
Tel: (0)1246 854268
Family-run display herb gardens
and nursery. Cold exposed site,
so there's a good display of
hardy herbs. Cafe and shop.
Located close to Hardwick Hall.

The Herb Nursery
Thistleton
Oakham
Rutland LE15 7RE.
Tel: (0)1572 767658
Well-established herb nursery
with display gardens. It
specializes in scented geraniums.

Hestercombe Gardens
Cheddon Fitzpaine
Taunton
Somerset TA2 8LQ
www.hestercombegardens.com
Both 18th- and 20th-century
gardens. Note naturalized
wall plantings of lavender,
santolina, etc., designed by
Gertrude Jekyll.

Hidcote Manor
Hidcote Bartrim
Chipping Camden
Gloucestershire GL55 6LR
www.nationaltrust.org.uk
Inter-war owner-designer
garden superbly maintained.
Great topiary, good colour.
Dramatic and expansive.

Hintlesham Hall
Hintlesham
Ipswich
Suffolk IP8 3NS
www.hintleshamhall.com
Excellent hotel with herb
garden designed by Beth Chatto
for Robert Carrier.

The Manor
Hemingford Grey
Huntingdon
Cambridgeshire PE28 9BN
www.greenknowe.co.uk
Lucy Boston's creation and
inspiration for her *Green Knowe*
children's stories. Exuberant
English gardening.

Museum of Garden History
St Mary at Lambeth
Lambeth Palace Road
London SE1 7LB
www.museumgardenhistory.org
Small garden immaculately
tended, and full of ideas. Plants
all grown by the Tradescant
family in the 17th century.
Proves good ideas are ageless.

Norfolk Herbs
Blackberry Farm
Dillington, Gressenhall
Dereham
Norfolk NR19 2QD
www.norfolkherbs.co.uk
Gardens designed to
demonstrate herbs.
Excellent nursery.

Norfolk Lavender
Caley Mill
Heacham
Norfolk PE31 7JE
www.norfolk-lavender.co.uk
Lavender and more lavender
in traditional and modern
settings. National collection
of lavender, herbs, and other
scented plants.

Penshurst Place
Penshurst
Tonbridge
Kent TN11 8DG
www.penshurstplace.com
A host of gardens by different
designers. Borders, formal,
water, and naturalized gardens.

Reads Nursery
Hales Hall
Loddon
Norfolk NR14 6QW
www.readsnursery.co.uk
Display gardens. Nursery for
conservatory plants, fruits
and nuts, wall shrubs,
scented and aromatic plants.
Topiary.

RHS Garden Wisley
Wisley
Woking
Surrey GU23 6QB
www.rhs.org.uk
Flagship garden for the Royal
Horticultural Society.
Demonstrates garden designs,
skills and practice.

Royal Botanic Gardens
Kew
Richmond
Surrey TW9 3AB
www.rbgkew.org.uk
Research and ornamental
gardens. Discover new plants,
clearly labelled, and well
grown. Extend your knowledge
and stimulate the imagination.

The Romantic Garden
Swannington
Norwich
Norfolk NR9 5NW
www.romantic-garden-
nursery.co.uk
Gardens and nursery. Half
hardy and conservatory, *Buxus*
topiary, ornamental standards,
large specimen trees, and shrubs.

Sissinghurst Castle
Sissinghurst
Cranbrook
Kent TN17 2AB
www.nationaltrust.org.uk
Architectural and living
formality enclosing voluptuous
planting. Impeccably labelled.
Inspirational 20th-century
garden fusion.

Squerryes Court
Westerham
Kent TN16 1SJ
www.squerryes.co.uk
William and Mary house and
gardens in poetic symmetry.
Sage-filled hearts.

Sulgrave Manor
Sulgrave
Banbury
Northamptonshire OX17 2SD
www.herbsociety.co.uk
Headquarters of the Herb
Society. Herb garden
created in 2003. Courses
and events.

University Botanic Gardens
Trumpington Road
Cambridge CB2 1JF
www.botanic.cam.ac.uk
Beautiful and instructive with a
superb collection of lavenders.
Displays on plants and their
natural habitats.

Vann
Hambledon
Godalming
Surrey GU8 4EF
Tel: (0)1428 683413
Gardens developed from house
into woodland. Robust,
swathed pergola, superb
planted rill, naturalized wood.

Wenlock Priory
Much Wenlock
Shropshire
www.english-heritage.org.uk
Medieval ruins enhanced
by Victorian topiary and
new herb plantings.

West Dean Gardens
Chichester
West Sussex PO18 0Q2
www.westdean.org.uk
A Fine Arts centre, whose
gardens are equally decorative
and productive. Courses
and events.

Wyken Hall
Stanton
Suffolk IP31 2DW
Tel: (0)1359 250287
Series of small imaginative
gardens. Sensual and scented.
Nursery and excellent shop.

SCOTLAND
Drum Castle
Drumoak, Banchory
Aberdeenshire AB31 5EY
www.nts.org.uk
Walled garden replanted as a

history of the rose. 17–20th
centuries in four large designs

Leith Hall and Gardens
Kennethmont
Huntly AB54 4NQ
www.nts.org.uk
Massive plantings of perennials,
which drift up the landscape.
Sinuosity echoed in the
curvaceous hedging.

Little Sparta
Stonypath
Dunsyre
Lanark
A landscape inspired by
Classical and concrete poetry.
Contact Lanark Tourist Office
for details.

Royal Botanic Garden
20a Inverleith Row
Edinburgh EH3 5LR
www.rbge.org.uk
Wealth of plants and planting.
Pringle Garden specializes in
Chinese plants. Scented garden
near cafe.

IRELAND
Ballymaloe Cookery School Gardens
Shanagarry,
Midleton
County Cork
Tel: (0)21 646785
Formal garden of fruit,
vegetables, and herbs.
Great herbaceous borders
and yew maze.

National Botanic Gardens
Glasnevin
Dublin
Tel: (0)1 837 4388
Just a bus ride from Dublin
centre with over 20,000
different species and cultivars to
inspire in a variety of plantings.

FRANCE
Château de Chamerolles
45170 Chilleurs-aux-Bois
Le Loiret
www.loiret.com
New gardens and museum
to illustrate the history
of perfume. Grand use of
trellised arbours and tunnels.

Château de Valmer
Chancay
37210 Vouvray
Indre-et-Loire
Tel: (0)2 47 52 93 12
Surrounded by vineyards,
newly-created terraced gardens
with potager and scented
climbers on display.

Château de Villandry
37510, Villandry
Indre et Loire
www.villandry.fr
World-class potager in
Renaissance layout.
A perfection of clipped
box and symmetry.
Love and herb gardens.

Etablissements Botaniques
Latour-Marliac
47110 Le Temple sur Lot
Lot-et-Garonne
Tel: (0)5 53 01 08 05
Birthplace of the modern water
lily. Gardens and nursery for
water lilies and aquatic plants.

Jardin de Valloires
Abbaye de Valloires
80120 Argoules
Somme
Tel: (0)1 22 23 53 55
Opened in 1989 to display
plantsman Jean-Louis Cousin's
collection of over 3,000
varieties. Bizarre to
culinary plants styled
in island beds.

La Chattonière
37190 Azay-le-Rideau
Indre-et-Loire
www.lachattoniere.com
Nine gardens created since
1992. Ranging from
Intelligence to Abundance,
Science to Improbability.
Maturing well.

Musée de Cluny
6 place Paul Painlevé
750005 Paris
www.musee.moyenage.fr
Modern take on medieval
gardens. Planting inspired by
the museum's tapestries and
collections. Urban chic.

Prieure St-Michel
Crouttes
61120 Vimoutiers
Orne
Tel: (0)2 33 39 15 15
Ancient landscape redesigned
to echo history in a potager of
heritage vegetables, aromatic
and medicinal herbs. Modern
naturalistic and red gardens.

SPAIN
Alhambra and Generalife
Granada, Andalusia
Tel: 958 22 04 45
or: www.alhambra-patronat.es
A selection of the best-
preserved Moorish patio
gardens in western Europe.
Clipped myrtle and
manipulated water.

Jardín Botánico de Córdoba
Avenida Linneo
14004 Cordoba
Tel: 957 20 00 18
Created in 1987. Good research
source. Herb boundaries thrive
– notably rosemary. In May,
many private patio gardens
also open in Córdoba.

Museo de Sorolla
Paseo del General Martinez
Campos 37
Madrid
Tel: 91 310 15 84
Former home and studio of
post-impressionist Joaquín
Sorolla Bastida. Delightful
town-scale interpretation
of the Moorish garden.

Monestir de Pedralbes
Baixada del Monestir 9
08034 Barcelona
Catalonia
monestirpedralbes@mail.bcn.es
www.museothyssen.org
Triple cloister that has been
newly replanted with blocks
of lavender, thyme, iris, and
violets. Tilework, font,
and trees.

UNITED STATES OF AMERICA
The Herb Society of America
9019 Kirtland Chardon Road
Kirtland
Ohio 44094
www.herbsociety.org
There are Units throughout
the States that have created
or maintain herb gardens or
gardens with herbs. The
National Herb Garden is
within the United States
National Arboretum,
3501 New York Avenue NE,
Washington DC.
email: www.usna.usda.gov

Atlanta Botanical Garden
1345 Piedmont Avenue NE
Atlanta
GA 30309
www.atlantabotanicalgarden.org
Much new work recently
undertaken. Scented and
children's areas.

Briarwood Caroline Dormon
Nature Preserve
Natchitoches
LA 71457
Caroline Dorman saved and
grew Louisiana native flora,
then propagated and hybridized
it for gardeners. Native irises
and orchids are specialities.

Chanticleer
786 Church Road
Wayne
PA 19087
www.chanticleergarden.org
Some 12½ ha (31 acres) of
ongoing ideas. Sweet-smelling
herbs, woodland with exotic
groundcover, wild-flower
meadow, and courtyards.
Colourful and reactive.

Cleveland Botanical Garden
11030 East Boulevard
Cleveland, OH 44106
Tel: 216 664 3103
www.cbgarden,org
Headquarters of the Western
Reserve Herb Society. Mature
and well-maintained modern
herbal knot. Extensive library.

Hermann-Grima Historic House
820 St. Louis Street
New Orleans
LA 70112
Tel: 504 525 5661
In the heart of the French
Quarter, is a 19th-century
parterre with date line plants
and constant seasonal changes.

Ladew Topiary Gardens
3535 Jarrettsville Pike
Monkton MD 2111
www.ladewgardens.com
Superbly maintained collection
of topiary – including a
hunting scene, swans, gods,
and goddesses.

Landmark Society House
& Garden Tour
The Landmark Society of
New York
133 South Fitzhugh Street
Rochester NY 14608
Annual gardens tour of 19th-
and 20th-century homes and
gardens in early June.

Longwood Gardens
Route 1
PO Box 501
Kennett Square PA 19348-0501
Tel: (1) 610 388 1000
www.longwoodgardens.org
First-class gardens for all tastes.
Wide range of courses, tours,
and talks.

Michigan 4H Children's Garden
4700 South Hagadorn Road
Suite 220
East Lansing
Michigan 48823-5399
Some 60 themed gardens for
children to enjoy and explore.
Herbs in designs for a pizza,
rainbow, or dyeing cloth.

Toledo Botanical Garden
5403 Elmer Drive
Toledo
Ohio 43615
www.toledogarden.org
Founded in 1964. Tour herb,
vegetable, rose, pioneer, colour,
and cottage gardens. Gallery,
studios, courses, and talks.

Well-Sweep Herb Farm
317 Mt. Bethel Road
Port Murray, New Jersey 07865
www.wellsweep.com
Long-established herb garden
and nursery that has produced
new and improved varieties.
Excellent understanding of
growing conditions in the
United States.

Glossary

What's in a name?

This is a small selection of terms used in the book and in the plants' names. If you are searching for plants for a particular location – dry, shade, bog, or full sun – their names can provide a clue as to whether they will thrive.

angustifolia – having narrow leaves, varieties with this name have an elegant appearance

Artemisia – named in honour of Artemis (Diana), goddess of chastity, for the vermifuge, stimulant, and culinary wormwood family

cultivar – a cultivated variety – not seen in the wild

edulis – simply means edible; worth noting when creating an edible landscape

foetidus, -a, um – bad smelling; foetidissimus very bad smelling

fragrans – scented

fragrantissimus, -a, -um – very fragrant, also odoratus, -a, -um, meaning scented, and odoratissimus, highly scented

Lambrook – many geraniums and *Artemisia* spp. were grown and improved by Margery Fish at East Lambrook Manor in Somerset, England

lanata – woolly with a fine pubescence on stems and leaves; worth noting for evening and white gardens

Lavandula – the genus name for lavender, so *lavandulifolia* – lavender-like leaves,

lavandulaceus – lavender-violet in colour

luteus, -a, -um – yellow deriving from lutum, dyers greenweed, usually referring to yellow-flowering herbs

Nepeta, nepetoides – the leaf shape of the true catmint or catnip is replicated in a variety of other herbs and gives a "herb" look to the border

officinalis – means sold in shops; applied to plants believed to have medicinal properties

panicle – an indeterminate branched inflorescence

pratensis, -e – of the meadows; good for naturalizing

pubescent – covered with short fine hairs

Pulmonaria – from pulmo, the lung, because the spotted leaves look like a lung and they were believed to be efficacious for lung complaints. Interesting exponent of "Doctrine of Signatures" that plants indicate how they can be used by shape or position

rosmarinifolius, -a, -um – with leaves like rosemary not a member of rosemary; family – you get "the look" only

Salvia – from salvus, meaning safe, well, sound; the traditional herbal sages have excellent, beneficial, health-giving properties

Sanguisorba – from sanguis, blood and sorbeo, to soak up, describing the burnet's original use as a styptic

sativus, -a, -um – cultivated or improved, often for culinary use

Sawyers – Suffolk Herbs started at Sawyers Farm where they improved many annual and perennial herbs varieties, which are recalled in the epithet 'Sawyers', or 'Suffolk'

Sissinghurst – wide variety of specialist or improved herbs and plants associated with the famous gardens created by Harold Nicolson and Vita Sackville-West

sylvaticus, -a, -um; sylvester; sylvestris, -e – growing in the woods, forest-loving or wild; worth noting if you have a shady corner of the garden

Symphytum – the Latin, and common name comfrey; both stem from Greek and Latin words meaning to unite, repeated more graphically in the old English name Knitbone

tinctorius, -a, -um – for plants formerly used in dyeing, echoed in tinctus, -a, -um, meaning coloured

tomentose – covered with densely matted, short, rigid, woolly hairs

Tropaeolum – named from Greek for trophy; when trained up a post it looks like a Classical victorious trophy with round shields and golden helmets hung on a pillar

umbel – flat-topped inflorescence

veris – of the spring, as is vernalis, -e and vernus, -a, um

viridis – green also viridescens, becoming green; viridiflorus with green flowers; viridifolius green-leaved; viridifuscus green-brown; viridissimus very green; and viridulus somewhat green

vulgaris, -e; vulgatus, a-, -um – common, as in the common or original type

Well-Sweep – Cyrus and Louise Hyde founded their New Jersey Well-Sweep herb farm in 1960s and have since introduced new herb varieties carrying their name

whorl – when three or more leaves, flowers, or other organs are arranged around a node, e.g. bergamot or horehound

Index

Author's acknowledgments

My first thanks go to Marianne Majerus for not only taking most of the stunning photographs in this book but who also, knowing my enthusiasm for herbs, organized my initial introduction to my second recipient, Michèle Byam. Unfailingly good humoured and courteous, Michèle Byam has ensured that the writing, research, and presentation has been focused and enjoyable for me for which many thanks. A love of herbs and eating has created a wonderful friendship with Seiko Hirota with whom I voyaged around Japan's gardens and restaurants. Seiko Hirota is the possessor of a phenomenal global knowledge of herbs, which like all true geniuses she happily shares, thank you. Over the last decade members of the Herb Society of America have also introduced me to so much more than green leaves, especial thanks to Caroline Amidon, Joyce Brobst, and the late Joanna Reed. Finally, Jane Taylor for her energy and enthusiasm for my work and hers with children's gardens. Thanks must also go to Emma O'Neill for tracking down my wish list of images, Sarah Rock and Christian Küsters for the final look.

Final loving thanks to my family with their finely developed nostrils and palates for good smells and happy food.

Photographic acknowledgments

Mitchell Beazley would like to thank the following for their kind permission to reproduce the photographs in this book.

Key: t top b bottom c centre l left r right OPG Octopus Publishing Group

Front cover: t Marianne Majerus; c Harpur Garden Library/Jerry Harpur; b Marianne Majerus; Back cover: Jonathan Buckley; Spine: Jerry Pavia; Back inside flap: David Holmes
The following photographs were taken by Marianne Majerus: 2/Design: Caroline Holmes, Denham End Farm, 6-7/Design: Brita von Schoenaich, 9 t/Design: Schoenaich Rees, 10-11, 13/Design: Lesley Rosser, 14-15, 18/The Old Rectory, Kirby Beedon, 20/Holdenby House, 21 University of Cambridge Botanic Garden, 24-25 t, 26/Design: Caroline Holmes, Denham End Farm, 27, 30 t, 30 b, 31, 32, 36 b, 36-37 t, 39, 43, 44-45/West Dean Gardens, Sussex, 48, 49, 50-51, 54/Design: Nori & Sandra Pope, Hadspen Garden, 56 tr & 57/Ryton Organic Gardens, 58-59, 60, 63, 64-65, 66, 67 b/The Garden House, Buckland Monachorum, 70-71 t, 70-71 b, 72-73, 74, 75, 77, 78-79, 80 t, 80 b, 81/Glen Chantry, 82-83 t Barton Court, 82-83/b The Old Rectory, Kirby Beedon, 84-85/Helmingham Hall, 87 & 88-89/The Old Manor, Hemingford Grey, 90 b/Garden From The Desert, RHS Chelsea 2003, 94-95/Design: David Matzdorf, 96 t/Design: Barbara Schwartz, 96 b & 97/Design: Fiona Naylor, 98-99/Design: Caroline Holmes, Denham End Farm, 100 t, 101, 102/Sun House, Long Melford, 106-107 b, 108, 109, 110-111, 112, 113, 114-115/Elton Hall, 116 Hampton Court, Herefordshire, 118-119, 120-121, 121 br Design: Mark Brown,

122-123 t, 122-123 b, 124-125/Clinton Lodge, 130-131, 136-137/Manor Farm, Keisby, 139 b, 140-141/Design: Caroline Holmes, Denham End Farm
Additional acknowledgements: Nicola Browne 103; Jonathan Buckley 129/Design: Robin Green & Ralph Cade; Henri Carvallo 52-53; Coldsnap Photography 61; Pat Crocker, riversongherbals.com 127; Maj Curtis, Maumee Valley Herb Society 91; Helen Fickling 86/Design: Catherine Heatherington Designs; John Fielding Slide Library 142 b/Graham Rice; Roger Foley 100 b; Garden Exposures Photo Library/Andrea Jones 42; GardenPhotos.com/judy white 56 tl, 128, 133; Garden Picture Library Jerry Pavia 145 t & b, Howard Rice 1, 67 t, Janet Sorrell 144 b; GardenWorld Images 142 t, 146 t, 149 b; John Glover 34-35/Design: Chris Jacobson; Harpur Garden Library Jerry Harpur 28-29/Design: Teresa Chadwick, 33/Design: HRH Prince of Wales & Michael Miller for Porcelanosa, The Carpet Garden, 40-41/Design: Lawrence Johnson, 51 br/Design: Topher Delaney for Mrs Koppl, 55, 76/Design: Simon Hopkinson, 134-135/Design: Pascal Cribier for Marquise de Bagneux, Marcus Harpur 132; Naotaka Hirota 106-107 t; Caroline Holmes 90 t; Andrew Lawson 12/Ian Hamilton Finlay, Little Sparta, 143 b, 144 t, 146 b, 147 t & b; Dr Norman Lownds, Curator, Michigan 4-H Children's Garden 126, 139 t; Mise Au Point N & P Mioulane 104-105; Brian Oke 62; OPG Stephen Robson 19, 22-23, 38, 117/Penpergwm; Kurt Ott 9 b; Jerry Pavia 16-17, 138; Photos Horticultural 24-25 b, 143 t, 148 t & b, 149 t; Stephen Robson 5/Sooke Harbour House